THE INVERSION

THE INVERSION

How We Have Been Tricked into Perceiving a False Reality

Kingsley L. Dennis

AEON

First published in 2023 by
Aeon Books

British Library Cataloguing in Publication Data

A C.I.P. for this book is available from the British Library

ISBN-13: 978-1-80152-107-9

Typeset by Medlar Publishing Solutions Pvt Ltd, India

www.aeonbooks.co.uk

To the few

CONTENTS

INTRODUCTION

The only defence against these things is knowing about them.
If you know about them, you are protected ... But you must not
be idle about acquiring real knowledge of these things.

—Rudolf Steiner (1917)

It is a horrible fact in human life, that good is realized by means
of evil, truth by means of falsehood, beauty by means of ugli-
ness, freedom by means of violence.

—Nicolas Berdyaev, *The Realm of Spirit & The Realm of Caesar*

Things in life are not as they seem. As the Russian philosopher Nicolas
Berdyaev pointed out, matters in this realm are often established
through their contrary natures. These *contraries* may also be errors;
they may equally be reflections, or they might be intentional manipulations. It could be said that the human life experience has been turned
around and forced to face an existence increasingly unnatural to the
innate human condition. And this existence is established through what
is called the 'reality construct'. In each epoch, a particular reality construct is dominant, and this becomes the ruling consensus reality. These
dominant reality constructs shift over time, yet they maintain hold over

how each generation or culture comes to regard and perceive the milieu of their lives. And such lives, I argue, have now come to be lived as within a reversal. Within the pages of this book, I refer to this reversal as the *Inversion*.

Human life is lived as a normalisation of this inverted reality construct. That is why life is filled with so many irregularities, oddities, and downright madness. We all know, or instinctively feel, that something has gone astray. There is no reason to celebrate absurdity within our so-called 'celebrity cultures'. Or to accept the military-industrial-technological complex as the dominant force of political and economic governance. War profits the war mongers (and sellers), and plastic-people governments allow the corporate gain of pain. We live in a construct where competition is praised, and 'weakness' is shrugged off as an evolutionary pruning mechanism. We allow our young minds to be programmed by blatant forms of mental and behavioural conditioning, and we willingly accept our debt-controlled enslavement by continuing to pay into the prison banks. Things have always been weird upon the planet, but now things have gotten a whole lot weirder. Only lies prevail; pseudo-truths are what get votes. We now believe in anything because nothing seemingly has any truth to it. We've become lost within the reflections of our own mirror world. Seeing our reflections smile back at us, we are content with the distraction. Everything must be okay, we tell our reflections—the governments wouldn't lie to us, would they? We're protected by benevolent authoritative structures that care for us like our mothers. Oh dear. Topsy-turvy.

To let you in on a little secret—it's been like this for a long time. Only that until recently, the waking dream of the Inversion was good at keeping everyone asleep (except the rare few) because the trickle of consciousness within the reality construct was low. But something has been happening, if you haven't noticed? There's been cracks in the veil, and more consciousness has been seeping through. And it's been getting into our heads, even if we hadn't noticed. Gradually, people have been gaining more and more awareness over this thing they call the 'human condition'. There have been a few exceptional individuals within each generation that spoke about these things, or even wrote about them; but few people listened and fewer still read any of their writings (because they had been kept illiterate, for the most part). But still, the gradual seeping of consciousness into this reality construct continued. And the insights kept coming. Some people were inspired; others gained revelations. But the numbers remained small. The Inversion continued to impose itself; to keep the blinders on the dreamers whilst turning up the music. Greater distractions were offered; a glittering array of entertainment sprang up. And incentives were given to those people who began to open just one of their eyes. Those few who suspected something were spotted early on and fast-tracked up the hierarchy of the 'people pyramid' so that they benefited most from the pleasures and gains of the Inversion. Then these higher-ups would want to invest in keeping the system exactly how it was—a protection of self-interests. The masses of dreamers—the sleeping mob as they were called—remained swaying to the lullaby. But slowly, the frequency of the lullaby was being changed. A new vibration was being added. I think you get the gist of where this is going.

And it arrives to here: where you are sitting right now.

There is little time left for us to be idle. By facing some perhaps distasteful truths (or at least potential truths) we can be equipped with the necessary resources. For humanity to develop further, it must now face friction. Without friction, we may be facing a period of stagnation. In fact, there are forces within the Inversion that are pushing for a reversal in humanity's development. I refer to these aspects in this book as the *entropic forces*. Within the Inversion there are many examples of these reversals.

It is well known, for instance, that the inverted pentacle is used in black magic rituals, whereas the upright pentacle (see Leonardo's 'Vitruvian Man') is a sign for the correct orientation of the moral forces at work in the human being. Similarly, the symbol of the *swastika* (a Sanskrit word meaning 'well-being') has been used throughout the world in spiritual and religious contexts and is generally regarded as representing the power and energy of the sun. Yet its symbolism was inverted by the Nazi Party to be aligned with aspects of the Black Sun. Inversion techniques and strategies are going on all the time. In the past, a mystic or 'truth-speaker' would be turned into a heretic so as to invalidate their message. Today's version, the whistle-blower, is turned into a traitor and incarcerated. Puppet politicians are presented as heroes; pop-slaves as cultural icons; and tech-gurus as salvationist good Samaritans. The list goes on … peace is inverted into anti-war so that the war energy remains embedded. Debt is reversed into credit, so everyone thinks they have economic freedom. The list goes on and on … Again, I think you get the gist of where this is going.

It comes to here. It comes to us. And humanity has arrived at a point where it is embedded in deep materialism and is set to go deeper unless there is a move into greater conscious awareness. The *machinic impulse* is an extension of this so-far largely unquestioned myth of materialism. The human narrative, by placing materiality as primary, has created for itself a path that leads into a machinic future. And the social-cultural systems that are emerging to bring in this machinic future are orientated towards technocracy. The primacy of materialism has unfolded these events. Yet they do not need to become the human future. If there is a recognition of the primacy of consciousness, then the game plan changes. It is the agenda of the Inversion to get everyone enthralled with the game of life in reverse—and this reverse mode has the primacy of materiality as its foundation. If people could awaken their perceptions and understand more of the situation they are in, they would be less susceptible to the manipulations at hand. And when the true meaning of earthly events on the outer plane is understood—the recognition that politics, the economy, the culture industry, etc.—are like shadows cast against the wall of the cave, then real transformation is possible. Until then, humankind remains within the spectacle of an inverted reality construct. Yet that same construct is dismantling—and dismantling rapidly.

Stability is an illusion that comes from both our short-term lives and the larger tapestry of what we call history. The ship of civilisation has, it seems, been recently splintering into driftwood; and various parties are vying to grasp onto a floating piece. People are adrift too, and there are few life buoys in sight (that is, if you are looking through an external gaze). The crises that are erupting are part of the irrational make-up of life in reverse (aka the Inversion). I feel it is important to know where we are, and what's about our feet. That is why I ventured to write this book.

This book has been written to offer the discerning few a potential Ariadne's thread. Within these pages there are nudges—but not final answers. The reader must seek these out for themselves. There is work to be done. Yet the first step upon the long journey home is to recognise the place where we are each standing right now. Know your location; from this, you will have a better orientation of the next step to take. One step at a time—and watch out for those *false exits*!

The caravan moves on …

PROLOGUE—A BEDTIME STORY

We are dreaming the wrong dreams.

—Anon

Human life is a story. And yet it is not one single story. It is an open book full of rich, amazing, powerful, and sometimes dangerous, stories. Humanity is quite literally living its own *One Thousand and One Nights*, yet across millennia. And just like that book of masterful storytelling, there have been incredible stories that filled the minds, and hearts, of many millions of people throughout the ages. We live upon, and within, a story each second of our lives. Some of these stories are greater than others—more epic, more powerful, and more influential. Others are daily stories that fill our pockets and arrange our hours. Yet over and above our stories there has always been a grand narrative. It is this grand, sweeping story that narrates, and influences, the general direction in which humanity moves. And this grand narrative is often so compelling, so full of persuasive detail, that we believe in it wholeheartedly. Like an amazing tale told to a child before bedtime, this tale then becomes woven into that night's dream. Upon waking, the dream feels so real that it lingers far long into the day and until it is replenished once again before bedtime. And yet sometimes, within special circumstances, the dream is so captivating and so convincing that it causes the dreamer never to awaken. The dreamer continues to dream the dream that they were told before sleeping.

Human history is like a dream within a dream—an inversion within an illusion. And as many dreamers know, there are levels within dreams.[1] Like a Russian Matryoshka doll, there are nesting layers of stories that all combine to create an overarching narrative body or realm. And many people, like good dreamers, find themselves caught up within one of the layers. And it can be almost impossible to get out. Even though we are technically awake, we are also dreaming. Why? Because we are living through particular stories and narratives that have been sown, implanted, or entwined into our heads. They get into our subconscious, and from that privileged position they begin to influence our behaviour and thinking from behind the scenes. Even when we think we are awake, we are never free from those stories, narratives, and constructs that manage our perceptions and create the arc of our dreaming lives. To truly be awake, a person would need to know how to drop all these stories and step out of the construct; that is, to turn themselves the right way up within the Inversion. This may actually have been achieved by a few people, yet it has always been considered something odd, esoteric, or mystical, to do so. Because, to the dreamers, anyone who steps out of the dream must be some weird eccentric, must they not? Or that is perhaps just how the main story goes.

The mainstream story doesn't like very much when dreamers—sorry, people—try to leave. Why would people want to leave when the story is so compelling? Overall, however, this is rarely a problem as so few people ever realise that it is all a dream within a dream, so the issue hardly ever comes up. So, shall we get back to our story?

Note

1. For a good example of this, see the film *Inception* (2010) by Christopher Nolan.

PART I

THE REVERSAL

We do not grasp that we are invisible. We do not realize that we are in a world of invisible people. We do not understand that life, before all other definitions of it, is a drama of the visible and the invisible.

—Maurice Nicoll, *Living Time*

CHAPTER 1

Hidden hands
(unknown landscapes)

It is as impossible to exercise freedom in an unreal world as it is to jump while you are falling.

—Colin Wilson, *The Outsider*

Life, or what we know to be our life, is not an even playing field. It may take a person years to come to the realisation that, in some way, the game of life is rigged. We always like to think that we know what's going on, even when we have the niggling suspicion that we don't. Life is a game of participation and players. And at various stages, a particular view, or perception, of life and reality is supported and promoted over and above any alternatives. And this chosen central narrative is made to seem reasonable to us, even when, upon closer examination, it is not. Everything we are told may appear reasonable initially because it is modelled, or programmed, to fit a very specific reality model. If our perceptions of reality were to shift, just a little, then we would see (or rather, perceive) that these current patterns of thinking are completely skewed. Yet the main consensus narrative story—or reality model—we adhere to keeps this skewed vision as a seemingly straight line. In this, most of the time we are unable to see, or we fail to see, the fundamental wrongness that lies at the heart of the main narrative. And this is the *Inversion*.

Of course, there have been people who from time to time attempted to point out these discrepancies. Many of them were ridiculed, persecuted, ostracised, or worse (and anything in-between). It would be fair to say that much of what passes for the mainstream dominant narrative—the human story—is an inversion. It can be said that the story we cling to is somehow topsy-turvy, or upside down. And from this topsy-turvy position it is very difficult to see things are they are, the right way up. The double disadvantage here is that the dreamer is not only dreaming within various levels but is also viewing the dream from the wrong side up. The act of dreaming is also inverted. Naturally, from this viewpoint it is hard to know what is right and wrong, or up or down. And it is very difficult to see the nature of this dreaming inversion precisely because it is propagated as normality. We don't know what we don't know. What we do know, however, is what we are told to know. And that is the nature of dream conditioning. Further, the inverted bandwidth we tend to be within is a tiny band of possibility. Anything beyond those bands is categorised and marked as abnormal, or *para*normal (meaning, beyond normal). What is in fact regarded as 'normal' is an extremely limiting range of the programmed story. And this normalcy is often then validated and generated by a person's own internal narrative. When the line between the thought and what is doing the thinking is erased, or blurred, then we come to believe that we *are* our thoughts. The first step to be taken is to recognise, and accept, that our experience of life is itself part of a larger collective narrative as much as it is part of one's individual story.

The larger collective story—that is, human history—is constructed from fragments that are collated and framed together. It is a mosaic that is attempting to be a whole, integrated picture. And yet, in order to fit the fragments together there are filters that function to place these pieces into a pre-arranged narrative. What is being put together by the grand notion of history is a work of fiction that is injected with enough fragments of facts to make the conditioned perspectives of the chroniclers seem plausible. Within this grand scheme of history lies the lesser groupings of cultural identities that bind us within further levels of the collective dreaming. The cultural story is yet another narrative fitted into the already narrow bandwidth of our perceptual dream story.

It would seem that humanity's motto is—'If something doesn't work, just do more of it'. The thinking patterns which have been dominant within humanity's dreamtime thus far have not been entirely successful.

And less so in recent times. The story which has brought us to where we are today is in need of a new storyline; something different—a new plot structure. Perhaps also a shift from third-person to first-person narrator in order to make it a more intimate experience. We need to know exactly what is going on in our character's heads. For several millennia, the human story has been given in the third-person narrator. There was the god-writer(s) penning the plot as its characters moved along the board. This was typified especially by the Greeks who conceived of their plethora of gods as seated atop Mount Olympus and playing their earthly avatars against one another. These Olympian gods wrote the human life story, and each person accepted that their fate and destiny had been pre-written into the story. This narrative form has unfolded over aeons of human history into a plot device that sees the physical human being as connected with their writer-god 'out there', beyond the pages.

The notion of a divinely appointed kingship goes back thousands of years. This system was highly evolved during the long dynasty of ancient Egyptian civilisation. Interbreeding bloodlines between author(s) and characters created generations of so-called 'divine' rulers that played their parts within the story. Divinely ordained rulers were then surrounded by the characters of the elite priesthood. From this, the story of theocracy was born that saw a system of political governance and power as ruling in the name of the writer-god(s). This plot inevitably creates a ruling elite structure where the 'righteous' few are deemed as being part-possessors to the grand, sacred story. Such sacred, or divine, authority then becomes a resident feature of human governance. This channel of governance not only manages social and cultural affairs, but also shapes the mental constructs and emotional beliefs that become the dominant narrative. That is, a story gets adopted as the central narrative, which then becomes generally known as human history (this is the same as a storyline that becomes the central thread in a game structure). What has been fashioned from the fragments of certain constructs is 'his story'—a writer's creative licence to turn a particular myth, or myths, into a story written on a stone tablet, and thus set into stone. The Inversion then seems plausible.

As comparative mythologist John Lamb Lash has pointed out, the notion of a 'divine ruler-king' is what many early gnostic thinkers warned against as a form of *anomia*—deviance. In other words, it represented a delusional way of thinking, or a glitch in the human psyche. Another translation of *anomia* would be 'anomalous', suggesting it as an irregularity or an anomaly to the natural way of the human being. This anomaly or delusion of divine rulership was quickly vetted with political power and then surrounded and supported by a group of vested interests. Any original or archaic sense of sacred rulership was soon supplanted by an institutional form of social-religious-political power. This was initially backed by the inviolable hand of divine authority. It has since been passed on to a structure of Statism and pseudo-monarchism that itself has been superseded by an invisible, and largely untouchable, network of elites. The hidden hands have always been pulling the strings out of view. And it is these strings which pluck the chords of our human storytelling. The ultimate aim of these 'hidden hands' is for control of the dreaming mind—and the phenomenal world is the world of the dreaming mind. And it is this dreaming—the simulation of life—that sustains the life we know of in the Inversion.

The most efficient way to attract the mind of the dreamer is through images. Image-stories are what most influence and attract a society's development, as if the future *bends* toward the most dominant image that portrays its future. A dominant story acts as a magnetic attractor for the sub-narratives, and lesser reality concepts, to be drawn into a specific perceptual and material construct. In this, images become as rituals.

The image as ritual

The famous mythologist Joseph Campbell put forth five significant functions that need to be fulfilled by image-stories and/or the rituals of a society. These he named as: mystical, cosmological, sociological, psychological, and editorial. In short, *mystical* applies to a sense of meaning and the meaningfulness of the experiences realised by members of a society. *Cosmological* presents images of the universe and gives a broader structure to the understanding of human life. *Sociological* supports, validates, and enforces the local social order, including its rituals, myths, and inclusive societal norms. *Psychological* is what guides people through their lives, giving them teachings and education, and rites of passage. And finally, *editorial* functions to give definitions to reality constructs, and to shape perceptions and perspectives. Campbell later added two additional functions that were the political and the magical. *Political* validates the authority of certain claims and roles; and *magical* validates some of the rituals performed within the society.

In the 'modern epoch', however, these functions have become distorted from their original positions. The mystical has been neglected as profound meaning and enchantment has become lost, and 'spiritual' or religious enterprises are now more social than soulful. The cosmological has been transplanted by science and technology that, in its turn, has become embedded into mechanisation, power, and control—the machinic impulse and instrumental power, as I discuss later. The sociological has been transformed into bureaucratic administration rather than the mythic or ritualistic. The psychological has become an institutionalised form of mass hypnosis that prepares people solely to be 'efficient members' of society (oversocialisation). And the editorial function—similar to the role of a story or book editor—was once represented by the Church, then the Scientific Establishment, then the governmental body, and now has apparently fallen into the hidden hands of a technocratic elite.

The dominant issues that underlay many of these image-stories consist of: free will, good and evil, human versus Nature, mind versus matter, immortality versus mortality, individual versus collective, evolution and progress, morality and ethics—and now, human versus machine. The notion of human free will, central to the dreamer's story, has gone from the divine god(s) and anointed rulership to science and social governing, and now to progress and technology. All in all, it can be seen by the above trends that the movement in the story has been from one of cosmic participation to a story of mechanisation, automation, and an advancing technologisation of humanity; thus, furthering its separation from the organic background of life. As I later discuss, this is a shift into forces of the machinic impulse. The dominant pattern now is the accelerating emergence of technological forces that, by their intrinsic nature, imply core features of a new story. Yet, of some concern is that these new features also expand upon various existing aspects that are not now amenable to our human story. These aspects include: the rationalistic, mechanistic, individualistic (priority of self), and materialistic. These forces largely support and validate an economic story where ongoing material progress and growth are primary drivers. It is a dream of ongoing accumulation that has produced not equilibrium but its opposite, dissonance, exhaustion, and psychic fragmentation. It is a story that has been in slow burn to influence not only a machinic-material projection of consciousness but also, importantly, a form of machinic unconscious.

The issue concerning the leading, dominant story is that it rapidly becomes the image that creates the emerging living environment. If you wish to influence the future of human life, then you start early to control and manage the story it sets itself—or the story it takes on board and assimilates as its own. The technological image of humankind, in its modern form, has been in gestation since the throes of the Industrial Revolution. It was impregnated in the First Industrial Revolution; began its growth within the womb during the Second Industrial Revolution; started its passage through the birth canal during the Third Industrial Revolution; and it is now being birthed by the digital midwife as the Fourth Industrial Revolution.[1] Whilst there are many who celebrate this birth, it should also be noted that the technological imperative has become divorced from any meaning of human well-being. The cult of efficiency—the machinic deity—is now the ruling imperative. And with efficiency comes monitoring, regulation, management, and control.

When there is too much of a discrepancy, or mismatch, between the dominant story(ies) and the lived experience on the ground, then this is where social disruption and upheaval occur. It is therefore in the interests of those forces governing our human societies to make sure there is as little divergence as possible. What is within the dreaming minds of the people must match as closely as possible to their life experience, and for each to feed into the other so as to sustain the waking dream. And this brings us to a dilemma regarding the techno-digital future. By its in-built design imperatives, the techno-future will be forever running away from us (if we are not extremely careful, which generally we are not). Through AI (artificial intelligence), deep learning, and quantum computation, for example, the techno-realm will not only be re-designing and propagating itself beyond human understanding, it will also be developing an infrastructure and digital realm (a Metaverse dreamscape) beyond the human capacity to grasp it. This threshold where human capacity can reach or see no further has been labelled by the tech-commentators as the 'Technological Singularity'.[2] If the future beyond this threshold is also beyond the human capacity to envision, or grasp, and gain meaning from the story, then the Inversion becomes less a participatory story and more of an entrapment within another's story. The question facing humanity here is whether, collectively and individually, there is any resistance against this loss of story. A major influence on this factor is whether the individual feels there is any significant meaning and purpose in their own story in these current times. If there is an increasing loss of individual meaning within the incumbent dominant story, then there will be less resistance to moving into another's incoming story. For what will be the difference, people may ask, if there is already no meaning in the story we are living now? This is all part of the play in controlling the dreaming mind—the collective Inversion—and relates to what I will discuss regarding the dissociation in the modern psyche.

It is said that a meaningful existence in life is derived through the relationships between oneself, society (social relations), and to the larger cosmos. All these elements are also part of the dreaming story and should not stand apart from it. The image that humanity has had of itself has always been derived externally. The grander story arc that perpetuates the Inversion has always triggered the individual's own sense of themselves. It is, then, a personal story-image constructed from influences of the external narrative that have been filtered and internalised. What has been lacking is a degree of self-reflection that can produce, develop, and nurture one's own story within the greater dream. And that is why many a wisdom tradition has used the rallying cry of 'Awake, dreamer—awake!'

So far, almost all individual 'awakening' or increase in self-awareness has only led to a person being more integrated into the consensus narrative. Rather than establishing a way out of the dream, many individual forms of awakening (or so-called 'awakenings') have further stimulated a sense of participation, albeit slightly different from the 'just a cog-in-the-machine' perspective. And yet these deeper modes of participation only serve to reinforce and validate the dominant consensus story narrative. Within the Inversion, the social order must be maintained at all costs, which means that the genuine mystical imperative to *transcend the social order* is not tolerated as it would entail breaking away from the control systems of the Inversion. The inner drive for transcendence—or awakening from the dream-state—is actually disruptive and in opposition to the controlled apparatus. Hence, such drives need to be redirected and managed through various strategies of socio-spiritual engineering, as I discuss in a later chapter. Be aware, the 'eccentric mystic' cannot be allowed to infect the masses—transcendence may be contagious. It is for this reason that most social authorities not only tolerate but are seen to encourage sanctioned paths of commercial 'self-development' as it reinforces containment in the Inversion for most practitioners. It is only the few who get away.

Most social revolutions have aimed at, and some have been successful, in usurping the governing status quo and changing the sub-story. And yet, the overarching dreamtime story stays in place. There has been a scene change within one of the acts; some of the characters have exited the stage and new ones have arrived. Yet the play remains a play—and all the world's a stage (as Shakespeare famously said). Or, to use more modern terminology: the programmes are swapped but the metaprogrammes remain. In other words, most cultural transformations either bring in an adapted form of the earlier dominant narrative, or usher in a new dream narrative for the epoch. And yet in each case, the dreaming consciousness of humanity remains. The Inversion evolves, and heightened perception of consciousness is overlooked (or intentionally neglected).

Which story will win over and gain dominance first? Or perhaps the future will be split between differing dominant stories, such as social realisation (techno-future) and self-realisation (human-centric future). It may also be a hesitant relationship between what is tolerable and what is desirable; also, between that which is restorative and that which is manipulative. A significant element that may work in the dreamer's favour is that almost all stories, especially dominant narrative ones, inevitably contain their own anomalies. And these anomalies can be fundamental to the underlying function of the main narrative. No story is ever 100 per cent water-tight—ask any storyteller! In our case here, the anomalies are most often related to the unpredictable, yet immensely creative and resilient, presence of the human being. And sometimes, it may be that the 'hidden hands' have utilised stories so that the herds don't go racing off the cliffs like lemmings or become victims of their own worst nightmares.

Because the genuine human story is missing here, there is a non-visible but unmissable hole within the dreamer's heart. It may be fair to say that, speaking generally, the dreamer is a wounded dreamer. Some stories may have served as counterbalances to this lack of wholeness. Human evolution needed to ensure the continuation of the species. Self-annihilation is never a good long-term future prospect. The religious impulse may be regarded, on one hand, as acting as an inhibiting factor against this annihilation, and as giving a background story to creation—the whys and therefore of existence. That is why virtually all cultures have their own origin stories and myths, whether they be gods or aliens. They bring to the narrative a point of origin from where the pen began to write the first words. However, stories with origins also feel more inclusive and contained—a perfect container for an overarching control system to be implanted within the inverted reality construct. It may be surmised that the evolutionary line of humanity within the Inversion dwells within a very sophisticated control programme that continues to be maintained across the planet by a few well-organised hidden hands.

Part of the narrative programming has led to a mindset of 'victim consciousness' that fosters a sense of incapacity and inability to resist external forces. Also, that there may be the hope of rescue or 'salvation' from these outside agents. These forms of external dependency have led, over time, to a weakening of personal responsibility, anxiety over leaving one's established comfort zones, and a fear of the unknown and uncertain. As researcher John Lamb Lash has noted, a form of 'Salvation history' has dominated the latter part of the Western religious narrative. Such Salvationism is 'embedded with a set of beliefs about creation, sin, sexuality, divine election, off-planet intervention, redemption, cosmic judgment, retribution, and resurrection. Such is the directive script for Western civilization'.[3] Lash considers this divine Salvationism as completely contrary to humanity's innate moral instincts; that is, it is an artificial narrative construct. Much of our institutionalised sacred history has come to be part responsible for the alienated nature of the human psyche. Like our biblical ancestors, we have been wandering in exile. Lash also notes that a communal form of collective psyche has held great power over the human mindset. In other words, a consensus story narrative has been responsible for birthing, or forming, our social systems, and the social management control structures that have arisen from this. It can be said that we have inherited a mythological mutation and now, like a loop pattern, we re-live this programming over and over again within the Inversion. What each individual needs is a form of psychic immunity, and yet so few people consider this as a necessity because so few recognise the issue. As Lash says: 'Unless there is internal force for resistance, psychic immunity, so to speak, the individual psyche will adapt to the stress of collective imagination. It will become what it believes and forget what it knows'.[4] Human history has long been a history of the power of the collective story (or programme) to hold individual minds captive, or captivated. And from this has arisen the great deception—the Inversion of a lesser reality.

Notes

1. See the World Economic Forum on this—www.weforum.org/agenda/ 2016/01/the-fourth-industrial-revolution-what-it-means-and-how-to-respond/
2. See especially the work *The Singularity is Near* by Ray Kurzweil.
3. John Lamb Lash, *Not In His Image: Gnostic Vision, Sacred Ecology, and the Future of Belief* (Vermont: Chelsea Green Publishing, 2006), 67.
4. John Lamb Lash, *Not In His Image: Gnostic Vision, Sacred Ecology, and the Future of Belief* (Vermont: Chelsea Green Publishing, 2006), 86.

CHAPTER 2

The inversion
(aka, The Great Deception)

Those who are able to see beyond the shadows and lies of their culture will never be understood, let alone believed, by the masses.

—Plato

As here I am discussing inversions, false realities, and distorted constructs, I will be making use and reference to the gnostic perspective and vision. As I discussed in my previous work—*Healing the Wounded Mind*—Gnosticism is an expression of a particular knowledge of reality. It is a form of direct-intuitive knowledge that transforms the human psyche and heightens the perceptual faculties. A genuine gnostic path is not a religious one, despite what some religious scholars may argue. Direct-intuitive knowledge provides information about the structure of reality, yet it does not provide 'Truth'. Instead, it provides the means whereby a person may break away from the dominant narrative and perceive beyond the reality construct. What this body of intuitive knowledge says is that the human being is not purely a material creature—a bio-physical complex made up of atoms—but is a vehicle for an indwelling spirit to maintain contact with Source. And this Source contact brings awareness beyond the normal range of perceptions. Gnosis is a direct

13

communion with Source, without the need for an intermediary agent or institution. A guide, or 'wayshower', may assist at specific times; yet final realisation is a personal, direct experiential knowing. Gnostic philosophy states that within each person resides a residual memory of wholeness. It is this residual memory that may be felt as a 'nagging' or 'urging' from deep within, as though we have forgotten something—as if we need to fulfil some promise that we made to ourselves. It is this which exists as the antidote to the mass mental programming that sustains the dreaming mind.

However, the individual is imbued with unconscious compulsions that act against the innate developmental potential. These counter-evolutionary forces have been given many names over the years—from djinn, devils, archons, aliens, hostile forces, and more. These forces that seek for psychic dominance over the individual can be regarded as *aspects of the Inversion* that aim to keep the dreaming mind from awakening to recognition of its captive state of limited awareness. The acknowledgement of these antagonistic forces in human life is also a part of the gnostic understanding. And this understanding takes evil seriously in that it recognises that there exist forces of 'psychic dominance'. This recognition is especially important for our current world, for such forces are not only more active but they are also more visible in their machinations. The gnostic perspective identifies these degenerative impulses at work. The sense of the 'alien mind'—or the alienation of human consciousness—must be felt and experienced before it can be recognised for what it is. Only then can the dreamer's mind view its own dreaming state. Or, in other words, the player can see that they are playing out a drama story written by another.

It may sound odd to say that there are 'shadowy forces' at play within this reality construct, yet careful consideration may reveal this to be the case. Is it not also the case that as soon as a person tries to delve too deeply into such investigations, distractive elements suddenly arise to throw a person off course? The forces of self-deception are likewise incredibly persuasive. Ignorance is no antidote; evasion that seeks refuge in transitory diversions and distractions is no solution. This is one reason why modern society is so 'diversion heavy' with its entertainments and commercial entrapments. The genie (djinn) is already out of the bottle, and they parade in front of us all the time with their flashy wares and hypnotic tricks. The great Inversion that is this reality construct (or reality simulation) uses a series of rituals to present itself.

And those who prefer to identify wholly with the physical-material world to the exclusion of the metaphysical are, in Gnostic terms, said to be inwardly dead. Perhaps this is one reason why current entertainments are filled with movies, TV series, and books about zombies and the walking dead. We have been staring ourselves in the face and we hadn't realised it. The joke is an open secret yet closed to most people's perceptions.

There is much mythological symbolism around death, dying, and journeys into the underworld. The dead must learn to come alive in life or they remain forever in a reality that is the dreaming world (Hades/ Hell?). The gnostic vision recognises the dark as well as the light. It sees both in operation and not necessarily in opposition. The polarities must be faced and not ignored. The shadows must be seen and identified, for it is through the darkness that the light comes in. Similarly, no healthy tree can disown its own roots that grow deep into the dark soil below. To do so would bring death. Life is also about being rooted in our own soils in order to gain awareness from within the dream. According to mythologist Joseph Campbell:

> It is not society that is to guide and save the creative hero, but precisely the reverse. And so every one of us shares the supreme ordeal—carries the cross of the redeemer—not in the bright moments of his tribes' great victories, but in the silences of his personal despair.[1]

The holy archetype of the redeemer is to bring creative energies through first knowing the darker shadows within the dreaming story.

The redeemer

There is a powerful concept here in the notion of the redeemer. Whilst the superficialities of the religious stories miss the point by upholding the idea of the god(s) as saving humanity, they misdirect from the notion of the individual being reborn through a death to self (ego death) to become their own redeemer. The story of inner realisation goes contrary to the idea, or ideology, of an external, interventionist god. The story narrative of the dreamer awakening—to 'die before you die'—had to be eliminated as a dangerous threat to the incumbent dominant narrative. The gnostic perspective considers the salvationist narrative to be a corruption. One of the reasons for this is that it establishes a victim consciousness among people; also, it debilitates individual free will. To be 'saved' by some form of external intervention leaves the human being without their own inherent and innate capacity to seek and nurture their own state of development. And yet, the reality construct does not wish that people become their own individual redeemers. For then, they would gain an inner authority and independence and would inevitably become guides and wayshowers for others.

The gnostic vision is not any specific doctrine or ideology; nor is it a fixed philosophy, and certainly not a dogma. It is a vision—a way of perceiving reality. As such, the gnostic vision is one that perceives the inversion of reality. The Gnostic is the person who perceives through the secondary and superficial layers of reality and into the deeper truths. It is like being hung upside down in the middle of a room—all the things you can see are upside down, are inverted. In Plato's famous analogy, only the shadows on the wall are seen, and not the primary source that creates the shadows. This inverted realm is the dreamer's world. The redeemer is that person, path, or guide, that helps to trigger a clarity of true awareness within the dreamer. In this sense, every dreamer secretly longs to be redeemed, even if they are not consciously aware of this. To be redeemed is to regain possession of something— and that is *oneself*. Or rather, one's innate connection with Source. This contact—this communion—is to be redeemed: re-claimed as one's true inheritance. The gnostic vision operates alongside this tradition of regaining humankind's original communion with Source. And to do this, a person first needs to recognise that they are dreaming. Secondly, to be aware of the forces that perpetuate and feed into this delusional dream, or inverted reality. Thirdly, to seek ways of transcending beyond the Inversion and into core clarity of perception.

The gnostic vision, alongside other wisdom traditions, recognises also that there are specific forces that act to maintain the Inversion, and to benefit from a sleeping humanity. These forces have been known by various names, according to time, place, and the people or tradition that is holding this knowledge. And yet, the ways, means, tactics, and objectives of these forces remain the same. Their aim is to deceive, manipulate, and—if possible—to control all the participants within the reality construct. And their principal strategy to achieve these goals is through mimicry. The simplest definition of mimicry is to imitate or copy someone or something, often with an aim in mind. In our context here, the copy is the fake version that takes the place of the real. As the Persian mystic Rumi stated: 'False gold exists because there is real gold'. The fake also serves to verify that the original exists. In modern vocabulary, we would refer to this 'fake version' or mimicry as a simulation or simulacra, which has been an increasing facet of contemporary life.[2] The forces of mimicry and delusion are imposters. The Gnostics referred to these forces as 'cosmic parasites' in that they leech off the energies and perceptions of human beings. Their greatest trickery is self-deception, for if the individual chooses to believe in the inverted reality—or replacement reality—then the work has been done for them. And then, we are deceived into investing in our own delusions. These forces are perpetually managing simulacra and thriving on simulated perceptions and an inverted human psychology. This is how they literally get 'into our heads' by getting us to do all the work of deluding ourselves. It is a very impressive strategy. And effective, too.

The preference for simulation rather than the Real sets a dangerous precedent for deviating away from the conscious evolution of humanity. The focus on replication over, and above, the Real is a sign of 'spiritual error'. This false narrative has created and sustained a construct of social domination and spiritual control that has become the dominant story for most of human civilisation. The gnostic perception is that these forces are in *error* rather than being evil. To say that they are evil suggests that not only should they not be a part of existence but that they are beyond redemption—beyond regaining contact with Source. And both of these suggestions are not true. Error is also a necessary component of existence, for its presence assists in validating that which is 'of truth'. Again, false gold exists in order to validate the worth of the real gold. The more there is false gold in circulation, the greater the value of the real gold. Further, errors allow people to make choices and sometimes compel, or push, people to navigate through these errors. Errors allow us to learn quicker than we would perhaps have otherwise. And this learning component is fundamental to the human life experience. These errors are therefore complementary to existence; and yet, they are also to be avoided when/if possible. If we succumb to these errors, and allow them to strengthen their presence, we place our own evolvement in great jeopardy for these *forces of error* are devolutionary, or entropic, forces.

The error

In the Gnostic Gospel of Philip, it is written: 'So long as the root of wickedness is hidden, it is strong. But when it is recognized, it is dissolved. When it is revealed, it perishes ... It is powerful because we have not recognized it' (II, 3, 83.5–30). The human being deviates because of the errors within their own minds. It is these that need to be recognised. To discern what is objectively Real, the dreamer must first learn to recognise what is false, and what is in error. The Real is veiled by that which deceives us. According to comparative mythologist John Lamb Lash, the gnostic perspective states three aspects of human error: i) humans are creatures who learn by making mistakes; ii) to learn from our mistakes we must detect and correct them; and iii) when we fail to detect and correct our mistakes they can extrapolate wildly and spin us beyond human limits.[3] The devolutionary, entropic forces are most effective, and active, at the point where we succumb to our errors; and they intervene to further compel a person to veer away from a path of potential awareness and awakening. Errors, it seems, are all part and parcel of the Inversion's dreaming narrative.

It is no accident that the narrative of modern life encourages people to develop a 'strong personality' and a robust 'self-identity' so as to 'get along' in the world and to rise through the competing masses. This selfish type of individualism is a sign of the times, which also serves to strengthen the personality-ego, thus driving a person further away from the clarity of perception. Within the dreaming mind, we are at risk of losing the connection to our inner mind. Again, in the words of Lash: 'Failing to own and evolve the intelligence innate to our species, we risk being deviated by another kind of mind, an artificial intelligence through which we become unreal to ourselves'.[4] The risk of this human loss to an artificial intelligence runs throughout this book as one of its central themes. The innate human sacredness that lies within the heart of each dreamer requires a certain degree of responsibility, for its access can become closed to us if we have succumbed too deeply to the Inversion.

The distractive forces of the Inversion are very adept at engaging in what we would consider as mind programming. Occult techniques that can be used for negative programming of the social mind are well known to many groups—and they pose a great risk. Within the state of the current reality construct, various forms of social engineering, psychic-occult rituals, and mind programming are occurring on a vast scale (some of which I discussed in my previous book, *Hijacking Reality*). Again, we come back to the notion of simulation/simulacra, and the very real issues of fake news, pseudo-events, deep-fakes, augmented reality, and the blurring of the lines between one story narrative and another. Even our standard physical senses are deceived, and so deceive us in turn. The 'errors' within the Inversion are disguised within our own thinking patterns. Anomalies, or deviances, are positioned in our minds. That is, we are implanted with *false minds*.

The gnostic visionaries created a body of work that put forth their cosmology; some of this material was later unearthed as the Nag Hammadi texts. Their cosmology explained how human life on this planet is under the influence of an intelligence—a 'god-imposter'—that seeks to maintain nefarious control over humanity through establishing a *reverse reality*. Hence, we have the Inversion. This intelligence, which the Gnostics called the Demiurge, is able to gain access and influence into this world through the mind of humanity. And through this influence, the Demiurge (and its sub-forces) aim to deceive humanity at all times. Further, there are many people in positions of power—from the priest-kings of old to the oligarchs of today—that have received support and 'energy forms' from these forces to evolve and strengthen controlling influences over humankind. These human factions have likewise sought positions of social-cultural and political-financial power upon the planet to sustain and manage this inverted reality construct. For in this, it gives them authoritative control, both physically and psychically. These controlling elements, say the Gnostics, are what continue to create the dominating narrative—and the 'dominator culture'—for the objective of furthering self-deception amongst the people. In this, people are programmed with false thinking patterns from the earliest periods in their life—from childhood onwards. If people were to change how they think, the forces of control would lose their domination. And yet, within the Inversion, we are persuaded from changing our minds.

People are also conditioned and persuaded from understanding their own inherent human capacities. This conditioning forces people to rely on, and become dependent upon, external agencies and bodies of social power; and this then distracts people from recognising their own innate abilities. Human cognition and perception is restricted and, in most cases, corrupted through false narratives and programming. The Demiurgic forces fear the recognition of true human potentialities and attempt to deny humanity access to their own means of perceptual development. These strategies give rise to forms of psychosocial control that, by their very nature, are insidious. In this, humanity inhabits a 'false realm'—the Inversion—that is in need of correcting its *errors*. Humanity has the inherent potential for its own evolution; yet, at the same time is vulnerable to the influence of deviant forces. In this, ignorance is our true error. The gnostic perspective, however, is not to place any blame but rather to offer a means of refocusing awareness and development towards a finer degree of perception. The gnostic vision seeks to gain knowledge about the workings of the Inversion and to turn this in the favour of the individual in realigning them toward a direct vis-à-vis relationship with Source. Knowing that we are deviated from the Greater Reality can also serve as a revelation to help us in finding our re-connection and re-alignment. The recognition of being lost is the very key to beginning the pursuit of genuine freedom. And yet, the recognition of our lostness is becoming increasingly more difficult as the Inversion accelerates its influence over us.

The Inversion has established a reality construct—an *inverted zone*—that has accustomed us to its environment and context. We have become, over time, more and more immersed within the story of the Inversion. And now the Inversion is advancing towards a realm of mechanisation—what I shall later refer to as the *machinic impulse*. We are within the machinations of the Inversion, and we don't yet know where the ride will take us. What some of us are sensing is that the current reality construct is reaching a stretching point, or moment of profound transition. We have always been travelling within the inverted zone; now, we may be beginning to merge and fuse within it. The dreamer has stepped into the dream of the mirror world.

Notes

1. Cited in Stephan A. Hoeller, *The Gnostic Jung and the Seven Sermons to the Dead* (Wheaton, IL: Quest Books, 2014), 113.
2. See my earlier book *Bardo Times: hyperreality, High-Velocity, Simulation, Automation, Mutation—A Hoax?*
3. John Lamb Lash, *Not In His Image: Gnostic Vision, Sacred Ecology, and the Future of Belief* (Vermont: Chelsea Green Publishing, 2006), 291.
4. John Lamb Lash, *Not In His Image: Gnostic Vision, Sacred Ecology, and the Future of Belief* (Vermont: Chelsea Green Publishing, 2006), 117.

CHAPTER 3

Mirror worlds
(fragmented landscapes and
high weirdness)

> Unless you know what the reality is, you will always tend to pursue the appearance.
>
> —Idries Shah

Reality as we perceive it is within an inverted state—or at least, this is the point I am making. Because of this condition, humanity views life as if through a mirror that projects back an upside-down reflection. Further, what we know to be our reality construct is splintering, since a purely material construct cannot maintain its existence indefinitely without connection and communion within a greater psychic unification. And from this, a gnostic-like awareness of being embedded in a 'reality construct' will increase as our technologies progressively intermediate the physical life experience. As outlined in the previous chapter, the gnostic vision shows that we occupy a counterfeit reality that veils our perception of the Greater Reality (the 'Real'). A counterfeit reality exists because there is another Reality on the flipside. One way to say this is that there is a 'false solidification' of the world based on counterfeit materiality—welcome to the *Inversion*. One person who understood this and spent his whole creative life trying to decipher it was the writer Philip K. Dick. In one of his later essays, written near the end of his life—'Cosmogony and Cosmology' (1978)—Dick attempted to put his gnostic understanding into a personal cosmology. His essay opens with the words:

> As to our reality being a projected framework—it appears to be a projection by an artifact, a computerlike teaching machine that guides, programmes, and generally controls us as we act without awareness of it within our projected world. The artifact, which I call Zebra, has 'created' (actually only projected) our reality as a sort of mirror or image of its maker, so that the maker can obtain thereby an objective standpoint to comprehend its own self.[1]

Dick viewed life as an evolving projected reality that is defective and 'malshaped'. And yet this very defectiveness was what compelled the human being to seek a merger, or assimilation, with the Source (or what Dick referred to as the 'Urgrund' after Jakob Böhme coined it the Absolute). In our current state, Dick considered that the individual already possessed fragments—or 'fractions'—of the Urgrund/Absolute/Source within them, and that the ultimate goal of a human life was to accomplish this human–Source merger: 'Already humans so closely approximate isomorphism with the Urgrund that the Urgrund can be born within a human being'.[2] In Dick's perspective, this Urgrund (Absolute—Source-of-All) was all the time penetrating into this false reality construct, and attempting either to trigger/activate people, or wait for them to awaken themselves, towards the time when a merger could be accomplished. After this merger (or 'Blitz' as Dick said, again using a term from the German mystic Jakob Böhme), the human being would have a perceptual comprehension of Reality that transcended all current temporal and spatial limits of the Inversion. If enough people were to assimilate with Source (the merger) then the artificial reality construct (the Inversion) would be annihilated. In its place would be a sentient reality-awareness that was simultaneously all within the Urgrund/Source.

Similar to the grander gnostic vision, Dick believed that the false god/Demiurge (or 'artefact') is not evil, and neither is the false projected world of the Demiurge. Rather, the Demiurge is 'ruthlessly deterministic and mechanical'. And in this, it cannot be appealed to. The Demiurge is itself an artefact that cannot fathom any greater truth beyond itself or purpose for being. It merely performs a function and is callously indifferent in this—this is the force that I later describe as the *machinic impulse*. This attitude is almost identical to those expressed by some contemporary tech-scientists who are working towards the actualisation of artificial intelligence (AI). They also believe that the coming AI is likely to be indifferent to human intelligence because it will be operating within a different reality construct (I discuss this more in later chapters). For Dick, reality must be regarded as a process that is moving towards the birth, or merger, of the Source within the human being. In the meantime, humans are compelled to suffer the pangs of pain that come with living within a seemingly indifferent cosmos. Dick's cosmology is a model that, as he says, suggests that our world is the attempt by a limited entity to create a copy—a mimicry. This would then account for the imperfections and the 'evil' elements contained within this reality construct. This model explains, according to Dick, the following facts:

1. the empirical world is not quite real, but only seemingly real;
2. its creator cannot be appealed to for a rectification or redress of these evils and imperfections;
3. the world is moving toward some kind of end state or goal, the nature of which is obscure, but the evolutionary aspect of the change states suggests a good and purposeful end state that has been designed by a sentient and benign proto-entity.[3]

In this schema, the Urgrund/Source-of-All and humanity is moving toward fusion whereby the intermediary entity (artefact-Demiurge) is moving toward final elimination.

Of course, this also begs the question that if the Demiurge gained a realisation of its own eventual demise, would it not seek cunning ways to avoid this? Perhaps the acceleration towards AI and a world techno-infrastructure is a means to sabotage this human–Source merger by further encapsulating the human being in an artificial, deceptive construct? I shall return to this theme again later. What Dick's cosmology does show is a form of evolutionary struggle, or contestation, between a natural evolutionary trajectory and an artificial devolutionary path. And within the reality construct, it is likely to be difficult to discern which pressures arise from the Demiurge—the artefact of *error* and falsity—and which from the Greater Reality of Source. This, it may be surmised, represents our ongoing human struggle in the polarity between 'good and evil', as it has been commonly depicted throughout millennia. Dick's cosmology also recognises this polarity struggle by saying that there is evidence that the Urgrund/Source does, from time to time, make a revelation to human beings in order to further the positive evolutionary process towards enlightened or perceptual knowing. And to counteract this impulse, the Demiurgic 'false god' entity would induce 'blindness or occlusion' to further the unknowing and perceptual darkness. This, argues Dick, is the perpetual struggle between 'knowing versus nonknowing'.

Regardless of all this, Dick confesses that he is pessimistic over the human future as the established artificial construct is just too good at doing what it does—it functions too well. Humans can therefore not rely solely on intervention to help them escape this false prison. They must also seek to activate the sacred spark within them. The rising must first come from within the individual if there is hope of meeting halfway the intervention of the Source from beyond the construct:

> Intervention in our world qua world will come only at the end times when the artifact and its tyrannical rule of us, its iron enslavement of us, is abolished. The Urgrund is real but far away. The artifact is real and very close, but has no ears to hear, no eyes to see, no soul to listen.[4]

The important aspect here is the recognition that within the current reality construct, the Inversion, there is an alternative non-visible realm of authentic reality. That such a truth exists, concealed by the projected reality or mirror world, would constitute, says Dick, the 'greatest esoteric knowledge that could be imagined'. Further, there is most likely to be unknown groups/organisations that guard the knowledge of such techniques that can trigger the perceptive awareness of this authentic reality (the 'Real').

Another significant point here, in this inverted mirror world—the reality of Dick's high weirdness—is the polarised struggle between liberation and enslavement: 'Inasmuch as the artifact enslaves men, without their even suspecting it, the artifact and its projected world can be said to be "hostile", which means devoted to enslavement, deception, and spiritual death'. Within the dreaming mind, life is artificially hostile to awakening and individualised liberation. And yet this state of affairs has become normalised within the dominant reality construct.

For this reason, we can say that reality is inverted as people are conditioned to accept their 'enslavement, deception, and spiritual death' as part of the regular way of life—and to not know it. The reality that is presented to us is a counterfeit one, and it is mightily effective. It is so effective, and efficient, that most people are not tempted to seek for any alternative. The coercive power of the Demiurgic dreaming mind is as penetrating as it is subtle. To affirm the existence of the Greater Reality, the person will have to deny the dominance of the consensus one. In the past, this has caused the denier much harassment, persecution, and even death. The dreaming construct does not gladly tolerate dissenters. Unless a person can reach a point where they can deny the reality construct through a form of initiation—'to die before you die'—then they remain entrapped within it for their whole life experience. Liberation thus requires a specific form of abandonment—a giving up of one's persona and the dominance of the egoic self. This has been considered part of the 'learning process' as a way to defeat the enslavement of the dream programming. Dick outlines several aspects necessary within this learning process:

1. We must recognize the existence of the artifact.
2. We must recognize the spuriousness of the empirical world, generated by the artifact.
3. We must grasp the fact that the artifact has by its world-projecting power enslaved us.
4. We must recognize the fact that the artifact, although enslaving us in a counterfeit world, is teaching us.
5. We must finally come to the point where we disobey our teacher—perhaps the most difficult moment in life, inasmuch as that teacher says, 'I will destroy you if you disobey me, and I would be morally right to do so, since I am your Creator'.[5]

By disobeying the 'teacher' (the false god), a person is denying the reality construct—and this is the whole point. Yet this is not an easy stage to arrive at, especially within a reality construct that throws so many distractions at the dreamer. Those people who benefit most from the artificial construct—through fame, wealth, pleasure, etc.—are the ones least likely to turn against it, and even less likely to deny it. What happens is that such dreamers make sustained efforts to maintain the reality construct, so as to secure their benefits. The Inversion is thus maintained from within by willing interests. The dreamers self-perpetuate the inverted dream for they are having pleasure, or take benefit, from its very existence.

Those persons less likely to benefit from the reality construct would be considered those most likely to question it. And yet this is not always the case. Such disgruntled people may question the unfairness of reality and its inequality, but on the whole this resistance takes place within the accepted reality paradigm. Something 'extra' is required for a person to consider seeking a vision, or transcendent view, beyond the dominant construct. Triggers from *beyond* the reality programme are necessary. What we 'see' and experience in this reality acts like a mirror. And a mirror can both reflect and deflect. It can reflect aspects that make us question what we see; it may give us a better angle to notice what is missing, or what may perhaps be the original source of the reflections. At the same time, the mirror deflects us from the origin, the original image, and bedazzles us with sparkling counterfeit images and distractions. This mirror world is the dreamer's world, and it is full of fragmented landscapes, high weirdness, and distorted perceptions.

The dreamer's dilemma

As Above, So Below. The dreamer is also a microcosmic reflection of the macrocosmic Source. Within the dreamer's inner being exists a reflection of the Real. The dreamer is also a shard, a fragment, of the Greater Reality—this also comprises part of the mirroring. Dick refers to this micro-macrocosm relationship as the following:

1. On the surface, the universe consists of a spurious projected reality, under which lies an authentic substratum of the divine. It is difficult to penetrate to this substratum.
2. On the surface, the human mind consists of a short-term limited ego that is born and dies and comprehends very little, but behind this human ego lies the divine infinitude of absolute mind. It is difficult to penetrate to this substratum.[6]

To penetrate into the realm of Source, it is the individual who must make the first active step. That is, the individual must make the initial effort to 'open themselves' to the influence of the Greater Reality. If not, any interventions from beyond the construct will only fall on deaf ears, or unfertile soil. The Inversion is a dream of separation and alienation; of having no direct contact with the Source of our being—with Origin. And this is the nature of the counterfeit mirror world. It is similar to light plunging into the darker density of water; it is refracted upon entry and the light ray appears twisted at an angle. We perceive this disloca- tion, this fracturing of light, without realising that it is a direct reflection from the origin (the Sun). In a similar way, we are not responding to the rays of light entering the dark density of our realm: *the Origin receives no reply*. The dreamer is asleep to the Call that has gone out.

The responsibility for the transmutation is upon each person. This is the difficulty, and the lesson, of being within the reality construct we call life. It represents both a separation—a splintering—as well as a longing. Within the present moment, we are also longing to return. The division is real and yet it is not. It can be said to be a *real illusion*. This is the dreamer's dilemma—the paradox within the programme. Dick speculated as part of his gnostic cosmology that the Urgrund (Source) was attempting to reach its objective by reflecting itself back onto itself, using the individual (in this case, Dick himself) as a point of reflection. We may consider ourselves as localised pinpoints of being that reflect the Source back to Source, and through developing this mutual com- munication a merger is achieved. Humanity can become a faithful and authentic reflection of Source, rather than the counterfeit dreamer's dis- torted reflection.

It is because of the innate reflective characteristics of the reality con- struct that we have in our realm the notion of polarity and polarisa- tion. Since this counterfeit reality is but a reflection/projection, it is not whole or complete in itself. This split from Origin is the very reason why this realm is defined and/or experienced through polarity—it is not unified. And since it is fractured off from the original Source, then by its very nature it is fractured within. These splinters are recognised through polarity relationships, which are themselves reflections of divi- sion and fragments of the whole. The Inversion is animated through the dynamism of opposing aspects or seeming opposites. These 'opposites' are themselves reflections of one another, just as the dreamer's existence is a reflection of Source. Within this realm of polarity, we sense intui- tively that we are strangers, that we do not belong—we are as *strang- ers in a strange land*. Yet if we confront the world directly, we become antagonistic to it. As an analogy, it is like we are wandering around as foreign entities within a host's body. Once we are awake and aware of this fact then we must continue to move around within the host in disguise, for were we to reveal our true origin then the host's antibodies would immediately view us as a danger and come to attack us. In this way, the artificial construct protects itself. And for now, we must do the same. If the dreamer awakens, they would do well to step lightly and carefully: to be 'in the world yet not of the world'.

Entanglement and attachment to the dreaming realm is only going to get deeper and more entrenched. The dense fog is becoming denser, aided by the acceleration of technological means to increase the hold, and control, of the artificial. The artificial is the antithesis of the Real. It is the jewel in the crown of the Inversion. The normalisation of this estrangement, which is the cause of much suffering, is the Demiurge's ultimate victory, says Dick:

> The victim colludes in his own suffering, and is willing to collude
> in a willingness to agree to the naturalness of suffering in general.
> Seeking to find a purpose in suffering is like seeking to find a pur-
> pose in a counterfeit coin.[7]

If we seek too long amidst the things of the unreal, we will eventually come to accept the counterfeit things as the end of our seeking. This is similar to the well-known joke of the drunk searching under the streetlight for his keys. A passer-by joins in the search and after a time of finding nothing, the passer-by asks if the drunk was sure he had dropped his keys here. 'Oh, no', replies the drunk. 'I dropped them over there in the park'. When the passer-by asks why the drunk is searching here, the drunk replies that there is more light here to see with. This once ancient tale has now become known in modern times as the 'streetlight effect' that signifies a type of observational bias that occurs when people are only willing to search for something where it is easiest to look. However, within the dreaming mind the easiest place to look is amongst the artifices of mimicry and within the counterfeit deceptions. This is the beguilement that sustains the trance of the Inversion. This is the marketplace that for too long has been selling our parts back to us. I shall leave the final words of this chapter to the late Philip K. Dick, gnostic unraveller and reveller: 'We got entangled in enchantment, a gingerbread cottage that beguiled us into enslavement and ruin'.[8]

Notes

1. Philip K. Dick, 'Cosmogeny and Cosmology', in *The Shifting Realities of Philip K. Dick: Selected Literary and Philosophical Writings*, ed. Lawrence Sutin (New York: Vintage Books, 1995), 281.
2. Philip K. Dick, 'Cosmogeny and Cosmology', in *The Shifting Realities of Philip K. Dick: Selected Literary and Philosophical Writings*, ed. Lawrence Sutin (New York: Vintage Books, 1995), 282.
3. Philip K. Dick, 'Cosmogeny and Cosmology', in *The Shifting Realities of Philip K. Dick: Selected Literary and Philosophical Writings*, ed. Lawrence Sutin (New York: Vintage Books, 1995), 284.
4. Philip K. Dick, 'Cosmogeny and Cosmology', in *The Shifting Realities of Philip K. Dick: Selected Literary and Philosophical Writings*, ed. Lawrence Sutin (New York: Vintage Books, 1995), 286.
5. Philip K. Dick, 'Cosmogeny and Cosmology', in *The Shifting Realities of Philip K. Dick: Selected Literary and Philosophical Writings*, ed. Lawrence Sutin (New York: Vintage Books, 1995), 291.
6. Philip K. Dick, 'Cosmogeny and Cosmology', in *The Shifting Realities of Philip K. Dick: Selected Literary and Philosophical Writings*, ed. Lawrence Sutin (New York: Vintage Books, 1995), 293.
7. Philip K. Dick, 'Cosmogeny and Cosmology', in *The Shifting Realities of Philip K. Dick: Selected Literary and Philosophical Writings*, ed. Lawrence Sutin (New York: Vintage Books, 1995), 307.
8. Philip K. Dick, 'Cosmogeny and Cosmology', in *The Shifting Realities of Philip K. Dick: Selected Literary and Philosophical Writings*, ed. Lawrence Sutin (New York: Vintage Books, 1995), 310.

CHAPTER 4

Normalised madness
(the upside-down world)

The condition of alienation, of being asleep, of being unconscious, of being out of one's mind, is the condition of the normal man. Society highly values its normal man.

—R. D. Laing, *The Politics of Experience*

Humanity has become a somewhat splintered species. We have splintered from our integral wholeness, and now find ourselves staggering around in various states of fracture. We have even become alienated from our own 'gods' who long ago seemingly left us to our own devices. Many have questioned: where have the gods gone? Fewer are those who have questioned where *we* might have gone to—or when it was that we started to leave ourselves behind? Humanity, in the modern age especially, appears to have become estranged from its own authenticity and its real possibilities. We have been 'othering' ourselves for centuries. Ever since the human species split from its sacred sense of transcendental connection, we have been living within a mass inverted mind that is estranged from the unified extended mind. We have been chasing our tails within the lesser reality of pseudo-events that distract our localised point of conscious awareness. This has led, after so many centuries, to a form of psychological dissociation, or trauma, within the human species. And what we are seeing around the world today is a form of this splintered psyche projected externally upon the fluctuating canvas of our inverted sense of reality. Some of this history has been recently investigated through the field of psycho-history (through the work of Lloyd deMause). Yet the specialised fields of psychiatry tend to focus on this as an individual problem or disturbance. However, the individual mind cannot be separated from the collective. It has never been separate—*only perceived as such*. As an example, episodes of inspiration or bouts of 'genius' can be said to occur when the localised consciousness somehow forms a bridge of communication with the extended mind and establishes an integrated whole—a *merging*. This is also mirrored within our own brain structure as the left-right brain integration. To use this analogy, it can be said that our localised points of conscious awareness (within the body) are processed by the left side of the brain, and a sense of greater connection and integration is processed by the right side of the brain.[1] And right now we are in need of integrating both parts to establish an integrated psyche.

This split of the human mind (from the extended mind and left-right integrated mind) has contributed to the perception of an inversion of reality—the mirror world's effect. As a result of this, we are experiencing the inversion of lesser reality in our localised minds. Unfortunately, it seems, there are forces and/or undisclosed groups that know of the Inversion and are exploiting it to keep us 'entrapped' or asleep within the lesser reality. Further, such groups are manipulating and engineering this inverted reality for their own twisted ends. Part of this agenda appears to support the arrival of a particular type of technocratic future—a technologised landscape that will further invert, or subvert, the position and role of the human being (the *machinic impulse*). Within such an environment, the human mind is likely to become even further splintered, or dissociated and disconnected, by it being intermediated by technology. Humanity is facing the danger of being closed off from the flow of unified consciousness that is the Greater Reality. If this is so, then it will lead to an extended and accelerated state of fragmentation of the human species.

I have written previously about how humanity may be experiencing a collective trauma on a global scale.[2] In that investigation, I proposed the possibility that some kind of mental and/or unconscious infection or contagion has produced a form of irrationality—or 'madness'—that has now become so normalised that we hardly recognise its presence.

Further, this 'normality' has embedded itself into diverse forms of social conditioning (or perhaps even produces this conditioning) in order to veil its existence. This *normalised madness* then usurps genuine thinking patterns, with the result that when everyone shares the collective psychosis then the madness of the world appears to be a normal feature of human civilisation. This corrupted mind, I would suggest, has now become the dominant narrative of the Inversion that influences social behaviour. This *disease of irrationality* is a contagion that infects individual and group minds as well as infusing the whole array of human social systems. It has been well documented—by experts within the Inversion!—that mental health in our modern societies has been declining for decades. This is indicated by a steady increase in the number of depression and anxiety issues, the number of suicides, and the huge rise in absenteeism due to psychological suffering and burnouts. A great deal of trauma is being experienced within people and within many of our human societies. What this suggests is that we may be heading to a tipping point where a psychological reorganisation of human life becomes imperative. In other words, reality is edging towards a shift into a new direction or phase, one way or another.

Life within the Inversion is maintained as a 'frictional experience' rather than a smooth one. We are told by various traditions and teachings that this friction is for us to gain 'life lessons' and developmental experiences. Again, this is the inverted thinking in action. What we are really experiencing on many occasions is a continuance of mini-crises. And when we have a situation that is a crisis, it is then only a small further step to turn a crisis into a trauma. When the trauma is related to a macro, expanded level—i.e. not just localised—then the very nature of that trauma is no longer an isolated experience but a continual process. Furthermore, a continual traumatic process only needs nudges placed at varying intervals to maintain, and sustain, the traumatic experience. The danger in this is that such an experience can be prolonged almost indefinitely if the nudges continue to be applied. In such prolonged states of induced trauma, as often is the case within the Inversion, it becomes very hard for a person to maintain balanced stability as they have become increasingly externalised and entangled in shared traumatic experiences. The Inversion then has programmes that deliver narratives and belief structures to create a sense of social solidarity—yet these are false paradigms. I have referred to this previously as the *normalisation of delusion*.[3] Through these strategies, a great deal of deliberate fracturing is established within human societies that then become mirrored in people's psychological states. This fracturing also causes a narrowing of peoples' focus onto a small fragment of the situation at the expense of perceiving the bigger picture. This orchestrated narrowing of focus breaks up overall awareness of reality into fractals—into 'reality bubbles'. These reality bubbles make it easier for manipulative forces operating within the Inversion to establish and steer mass psychologies.

The collective mass mind is continually being shaped by dominant social stories that normalise our mental and emotional behavioural patterns. These norms are then transferred into cultural myths that serve to transmit and reinforce these mass-minded belief systems. We end up validating our own corrupted thinking through unconscious affirmations. Once this seed of psychosis is planted then it aims to propagate and strengthen itself in order to legitimate its own logical existence. Like a mental cancer, it ingratiates itself into our own neural pathways as an insider rather than an *outsider* so that we fail to notice its toxic presence. Yet there remains a niggling sense of something being 'not-quite-right' at the back of many people's minds. It is as if we know, somewhere deep within us, that we are experiencing a reversal. And yet, everyone is the wrong way up—and so we are forced into accepting it as the normal. We adjust ourselves into a false consciousness that then adopts outer events as the 'true' and the 'normal'. In the words of the renowned psychiatrist R. D. Laing: 'What we call "normal" is a product of repression, denial, splitting, projection, introjection, and other forms of destructive action on experience. It is radically estranged from the structure of being'.[4]

This corrupted reality perception, or false consciousness, then becomes internalised so that people adapt to a form of the 'new normality' and anyone who speaks up or questions this 'paradigm of normality' is considered either odd, eccentric or, at worst, a crazy heretic. A more recent category for such people is now to be designated as a 'conspiracy theorist' which is a quick brush to dismiss people with ideas or thinking contrary to this 'norm'. And those people who appear to accept and encourage such norms are quickly brought into the fold and supported by the orthodox, mainstream systems. The majority of those supporting and propagating the *disease of irrationality* are not in psychiatric care but running most of our social, political, and financial institutions. A great majority of the asymptomatic, unknowing carriers of this mental contagion can also be found in the streets, in shops, and everywhere in society. Positions of great power especially represent this irrationality, and often knowingly so, as it supports and strengthens their own continuing structure of power. An irrational mind corrupts, yet an irrational mind in a position of power corrupts totally.

The irrational mind

The presence of the irrational mind is like a sickness of the soul, and it manifests as a disturbance in the collective unconscious. Just like any other virus or pathogen, it seeks to spread itself by infecting as many carriers as possible. Those people who carry the irrational mind (whether knowingly or not) act as transmitters and amplifiers for it, strengthening its frequency within the collective consciousness. A collective 'possession' can also be referred to as a psychic epidemic, or a disturbance in the mindfield. Such disturbances can affect and produce varying effects on people's mental health and well-being. Over time, this off-kilter mentality stabilises into a form of trauma which then is projected externally, only to be reflected back again—and the cycle continues.

People who suffer from this may carry it as an 'undefinable' trauma within them, and it is common to turn to alcoholism, hedonistic pursuits, addictions, and other dependencies as a way of coping, or escaping, from a sense of ennui, apathy, or plain world-weariness. When a person feels traumatised, they are vulnerable to further mental programming and varieties of external influence and persuasion. In other words, it is a form of shared, collective mental instability that maintains the Inversion in which most of us dwell. It can be very subtle too. Our modern societies have been stealthily constructed on ways to exploit this vulnerability to outside influence and persuasion. The result is that we unknowingly become bemused and increasingly strangers to our true selves, to one another, and to the realms of perception beyond the material world. Krishnamurti famously declared that: 'It is no measure of health to be well adjusted to a profoundly sick society'.

Individual traumas are given institutional sanction and support within a culture that has based its social norms upon such irrationalities. The irrational has implanted itself within our lesser reality as the 'rational standard rule'. It is perhaps little wonder that people are so susceptible to this mental corruption when it comes to us dressed up in sheep's clothing. As is always the case, those people most vulnerable are usually those who are conditioned to authority and obedience. This trait, unfortunately, is one that is first implanted through compulsory schooling. Likewise, people who are easily influenced by external opinions, and who are prone to group-thinking, are among the first to give away their mental independence to external sources. The irrational mind preys upon such group-think individuals as the mass mind of humanity helps in the transmission and proliferation of the psychic trauma. Again, citing the psychiatrist R. D. Laing:

> The condition of alienation, of being asleep, of being unconscious, of being out of one's mind, is the condition of the normal man. Society highly values its normal man. It educates children to lose themselves and to become absurd, and thus to be normal. Normal men have killed perhaps 100,000,000 of their fellow normal men in the last fifty years.[5]

If we are to gain a broader perspective on the human condition then it is important to view major events, human actions, propaganda, social disturbances, power struggles, and the rest, from the standpoint of the irrationality of the Inversion. Modern human thinking patterns have been conditioned around such traits as greed, competition, ambition, materialism, and selfishness. These are all traits that mark a lack of authenticity. The irrational mind seeks to develop greater degrees of inauthenticity and lack of empathy within the individual. The world stage is littered with such personalities.

The peril of the irrational mind is that resistance may also help to spread it. That is, people who start out resisting this corrupted mindset often find themselves adopting its values in order to survive. It is the 'if you can't beat them, join them' type of thinking. It seems that humanity is collectively struggling to awaken against its very own condition of traumatic sleep. It has often been said—by a small selection of 'awakened individuals'—that humanity is collectively asleep. The more we propagate the Inversion of the splintered mind, the more people will normalise their behaviour as automatons. We will live within a tighter range of conditioned stimuli that programmes specific opinions and thinking patterns which then validates the control of the irrational over us. The mystic-philosopher George Gurdjieff stated:

Contemporary culture requires automatons. And people are undoubtedly losing their acquired habits of independence and turning into automatons, into parts of machines ... Man is becoming a willing slave. He no longer needs chains. He begins to grow fond of his slavery, to be proud of it. And this is the most terrible thing that can happen to a man.[6]

By adopting the inverted reality of the mass mind, we are furthering our own behaviour of the automaton. And many of our incumbent social systems appear to be ready and willing to corroborate and reinforce such a consensus mindset. Our genuine awakening to this 'trauma of the Inversion' cannot come from any mass movement but only from those persons who can think and act independently.

Under the irrational dream spell

In his later years, the psychologist Carl Jung became increasingly aware of the dangers of mass psychosis and the psychic manipulation of the masses. Jung observed that the 'mass crushes out the insight and reflection that are still possible with the individual, and this necessarily leads to doctrinaire and authoritarian tyranny'.[7] And it was, he reflected, the minority elites that represented this tyranny. Regarding the mental pathology of the elite few:

Their chimerical ideas, sustained by fanatical resentment, appeal to the collective irrationality and find fruitful soil there; they express all those motives and resentments which lurk in more normal people under the cloak of reason and insight. They are, therefore, despite their small number in comparison with the population as a whole, dangerous as sources of infection precisely because the so-called normal person possesses only a limited degree of self-knowledge.[8]

This 'limited degree of self-knowledge' that Jung makes note of refers to the nature of the Inversion to keep people asleep to their true potential and entrapped within the consensus dreaming mind. The 'normal' attributes within the madness of the upside-down world are taken to be sanity for they are accepted, and regularly updated and redefined, by the ongoing dominant consensus narratives. And within this consensus agreement, everyone who adheres to this is considered as sane whereas those who question it, or attempt to step outside of it, are rendered as 'difficult', 'alternative', or 'heretical'.

The world of acceptance is at the same time a world of deceit. An unquestioning acceptance of the dreaming mind, and its internal mechanisms of conditioning and programming, are themselves acts of denial against the 'rightness' of reality. And for those who accept these conditions of the dreaming mind—which are the majority—are thus in self-denial, whether they know it or not. What this establishes within the Inversion is a world where its inhabitants are, on the whole, alienated from both themselves, and others. As Laing phrased it: 'Each of us is the other to the others'.[9] It is this othering which, contrary to appearances, supports mass-mindedness rather than genuine individualism. There is little doubt that anything other can be the case since the consensus dream-state requires mass agreement for its own validation. The human being, instead of being encouraged to live its own unique dreams, is being cajoled into living easily within the parameters of the dreaming reality itself. The subtext here is that people are cunningly persuaded to 'live their dreams' so long as they do so within the bubble of the Inversion. It is a form of diluted freedom that is only freedom within the allowed perimeter of the enclosure.

We are daily enclosed by the suffocating power of the masses that by their presence indirectly attempts to force upon us the insignificance of the individual. The tension and discomfort that some sensitive people feel is caused by an internal conflict between an innate connection to the transpersonal—to the *something beyond*—and the systems and programming that entangle them within the everyday mundane. This division is partly responsible for the increasing fragmentation within the modern psyche of humanity. To the attentive observer, it is apparent that citizens within modern societies are suffering from various states of mental dissociation, which in turn feeds into a collective mindfield of split consciousnesses. This, I suggest, is the ideal breeding ground for the dreaming mind to keep on dreaming. Almost everyone is playing on the same field without knowing the cost. As Jung aptly put it: 'The infantile dream-state of the mass man is so unrealistic that he never thinks to ask who is paying for this paradise'.[10] It is this 'dream-state of the mass man' that is part responsible for the elimination of the path of the individual. The inner need for individualisation is an assertion of one's localised expression of consciousness. And yet the dreaming mind neither cares for nor wishes to allow these localised expressions of aware consciousness. The collective dreaming mind wants only sleeping minds that it can further subjugate into the consensus dream-state. The madness of the upside-down world is a carefully orchestrated folly to eradicate the genuine individual. The Inversion then becomes the ideal breeding ground for establishing inverted mass psychologies.

The establishment of mass psychology

According to psychiatry, there are generally four conditions that allow for the easy establishment of mass psychology to emerge. These are: a lack of social bonds; people experiencing life as meaningless or senseless; free-floating anxiety; and free-floating frustration and aggression. In many modern human societies, these conditions have been building up for a long, long time. People swept up within a mass or crowd psychology tend to protect and maintain it whether consciously or unconsciously. This is why they are most likely to reject any contrary information when it is presented to them; or will reject even the chance for such information to be presented. This amounts to a state of mild induced hypnosis which has shifted from an external identification to a self-maintained state. That is, people engage in the process of their own induced hypnosis; this then further validates the nature of the Inversion. People who are most likely to accept the slippage into a mass psychology were already experiencing psychological discontent. Hence, life in the upside-down reality tends to maintain the friction of crises and mild, sustained trauma so that hypnotic states can continue to be induced.

Persons susceptible to mass psychology are less likely to be responsive or sensitive to rational argument and debate. It is because they did not fall into line with the main narrative through reasoning but rather through a form of 'mental intoxication' or irrationality that triggered a transference of social bonding to the newly established mass solidarity. Such triggers are generally most effective when they are presented through emotional states—these are often based upon fear; insecurities; and mortality. It is difficult to break or stop such collective psychological formations once they have been established. Once the psychological patterning and emotional identification has been constructed it is then difficult to deconstruct—a significant collective solidarity has been established that imprints the mass mind. Another factor that strengthens the mass psychology is that the imposed mainstream narratives that support the Inversion appear to speak in one collective voice. They are clearer in what they represent and appear to come from a place of unified agreement. These narratives generally belong to a well-thought-out programming that unfolds across local, national, and global reality constructs.

Those people caught within the mass programming of the Inversion believe themselves to be expressing their own opinions when in fact there has been a clever sleight-of-hand in that they have been provided with a set of pre-formed 'opinion bundles' that they can then put forward as their own. Such people are therefore not expressing personal opinions arrived at through individual critical questioning but rather conditioned 'thought bundles' provided through the programming techniques built into the establishment of the psychological collective mass. The mass hypnosis conjured throughout the Inversion comes with various pre-prepared collections of opinion sets for bulk dispersal. As Philip K. Dick would say, the 'artifact' has cleverly created its multi-layered programming for the maintenance of its artificial construct we call reality. Yet, within every programme there is in-built the potential for deprogramming.

The deprogramming of the individual

The astute and aware individual is the exception within the mass mind of the Inversion. The people who are generally less susceptible to the hypnosis of mass psychology tend to be those who disagree with the mainstream ideological programme or are more aware of the processes of social conditioning and the uses of mainstream propaganda. Yet most people remain unaware of the circumstances of their programming and retain strong belief in the controlled reality sets they are provided with. After all, it is a very sophisticated programme. By the time we are young adults, we are pretty much adapted to the madness of the upside-down world that forms our reality experience. This means, by our youth we are already fully immersed in the deception. We call this entrainment with deception as socialisation: 'Human beings seem to have an almost unlimited capacity to deceive themselves, and to deceive themselves into taking their own lives for truth. By such mystification, we achieve and sustain our adjustment, adaptation, socialization'.[11] The socialising imperative has largely been to organise a system of social engineering and control that can form, sustain, and manage the masses. At one point, this was called the name 'behaviourism' as spearheaded by the American psychologist B. F. Skinner. Skinner was famous (or infamous) for stipulating that human cultures should be intentionally designed for the control of human behaviour, and that this was a necessity for the human species to continue to develop. In this, Skinner declared it essential to abolish the path of individualism: 'What is being abolished is autonomous man—the inner man, the homunculus, the possessing demon, the man defended by the literatures of freedom and dignity. His abolition has been long overdue ...'[12] The abolition of the true individual was a necessary act of adaptation, reasoned Skinner, because a person does not act upon the world—rather, the world acts upon them. This reasoning was an important step for the later spread of the machinic impulse, as I discuss later.

Within the dreaming mind, individuals thrive better as collective organisms; and individualism is a threat to the status quo of the Inversion. This is emblematic of the drive towards creating the hive mind collective, as is explored in later chapters. Skinner, and behaviourism in general, believes that free will, freedom, and consciousness need to be reinterpreted and redefined in light of conditioned behaviours. The dramatic increase in the focus on managing human perceptions and the operant conditioning of human behaviour is a deliberate agenda for establishing 'psycho-civilised' societies within the current consensus reality. Psycho-civilised societies and cultures are predicated around the management and control of thinking patterns; that is, certain expressions of human consciousness. Modern life within the dreaming mind—the Inversion—is all about generating agenda-specific and goal-orientated narratives that steer societies, and their inhabitants, into desired directions. In this, the modern person is alienated from the instinctual foundation of their inner lives. They feel uprooted from themselves and without a 'home grounding'. This then leads to a loss of conscious knowledge of themselves. This separation further causes a conflict between the conscious and subconscious aspects—a split that can become pathological, according to Jung. This fracturing also reduces a person's sense of inner authority and self-authenticity. It erodes a sense of personal freedom, reducing perceptive coherence and capacity, leaving a person at a psychological disadvantage. The future, wrote Jung, will be 'decided neither by the threat of wild animals, nor by natural catastrophes, nor by the danger of worldwide epidemics, but simply and solely by the psychic changes in man'.[13]

The modern 'psycho-civilised' society has little interest in promoting conscious interrelations between people. On the contrary, it strives for the psychic isolation of the individual in terms of their true capacities, and the collective assimilation of the individual in terms of a carefully managed and controlled mass-mindedness. This is because it is the ability of consciousness, as exercised and expressed through the individual, that can break the perceptual bonds of the Inversion. In other words, with a correct attunement to consciousness, a person can awaken from the entrapment of the dreaming mind and perceive the Greater Reality beyond. The 'Great Sleep' of the dreaming mind is enacted through each person becoming conditioned, and then they unknowingly control others through the reciprocal effects of 'normalised' social relations. Another way to say this is that people inadvertently 'thought-police' control one another through such psychological processes as peer-pressure, group-think, and similar modes of social conformity. The inverted dreaming mind keeps on dreaming itself through the willing compliance of its dreamers.

Of course, external coercion is also necessary, and constantly applied, as dreamers have the habit of stirring in their dreams and becoming partially awake. So, the sleep sedatives need to be sustained and duly applied. As we shall see, the coming encroachment of technology's 'unreal machine' will have a great influence upon maintaining the Inversion. Another project also in this domain is the application of social fragmentation, conditioning, and trauma through spiritual control mechanisms and unidentified spectres.

Notes

1. See *The Master and His Emissary: The Divided Brain and the Making of the Western World* by Iain McGilchrist.
2. See *Healing the Wounded Mind: The Psychosis of the Modern World and the Search for the Self* (Clairview Books, 2019).
3. See *Hijacking Reality: the Reprogramming & Reorganization of Human Life* (Beautiful Traitor Books, 2021).
4. R. D. Laing, *The Politics of Experience & The Bird of Paradise* (London: Penguin Books, 1990), 23–24.

5. R. D. Laing, *The Politics of Experience & The Bird of Paradise* (London: Penguin Books, 1990), 24.

6. P. D. Ouspensky, *In Search of the Miraculous: Fragments of an Unknown Teaching* (London: Routledge & Kegan Paul, 1950), 316.

7. C. G. Jung, *The Undiscovered Self (with Symbols and The Interpretation of Dreams)* (Princeton, Princeton University Press, 2010), 3.

8. C. G. Jung, *The Undiscovered Self (with Symbols and The Interpretation of Dreams)* (Princeton, Princeton University Press, 2010), 4.

9. R. D. Laing, *The Politics of Experience & The Bird of Paradise* (London: Penguin Books, 1990), 26.

10. C. G. Jung, *The Undiscovered Self (with Symbols and The Interpretation of Dreams)* (Princeton: Princeton University Press, 2010), 33.

11. R. D. Laing, *The Politics of Experience & The Bird of Paradise* (London: Penguin Books, 1990), 61.

12. Cited in Shoshana Zuboff, *The Age of Surveillance Capitalism: The Fight for a Human Future at the New Frontier of Power* (London: Profile Books, 2019), 439.

13. C. G. Jung, *The Undiscovered Self (with Symbols and The Interpretation of Dreams)* (Princeton: Princeton University Press, 2010), 47.

CHAPTER 5

Unidentified spectres
(spiritual control mechanisms as trauma)

When a shattered psyche looks for symbols of wholeness outside of itself, it finds, inevitably perhaps, only the fragments of
a shattered mirror.
—Jasun Horsley, *Prisoner of Infinity: UFOs, Social Engineering,*
and the Psychology of Fragmentation

The Abyss has been looking into us for long enough. It is time
for us, after becoming as spiritually grounded and metaphysi-
cally well-informed as possible, to begin looking back into it,
and so come to a deeper understanding of exactly what is being
done to us—and maybe even who is doing it.
—Charles Upton, *The Alien Disclosure Deception:*
The Metaphysics of Social Engineering

Human consciousness has always been the prime target for mechanisms of conditioning. And consciousness can be affected through
both the hardware and the software. The hardware is the human brain
itself and its processing ability; and the software is the information/
messages within the stream of consciousness (ideas, beliefs, etc.). To use
an analogy for the hardware, it is like a virus aiming to attack and/or

unduly influence the hard drive of the computer. For if the hard drive is affected, then whatever software is processed through it will be partly, or wholly, corrupted. Similarly, if the information coming in (software) is already corrupted, then what comes out will be even more so. As the adage says: garbage in, garbage out (GIGO). Within the realm of the Inversion—or lesser reality—in which we currently dwell, there is a revolt against reality, as I have repeatedly pointed to. As of yet, humanity does not exist within a wholeness but rather amongst the fragments of a piecemeal story. These fragments are constantly rearranged to tell a different story according to time and place (the dominant narrative), and occasionally they fall from their allotted space and a gap appears. This is when we obtain glimpses 'through the veil'. The processes and expressions of human consciousness have almost always been the subject and site of deliberate management and conditioning.

In past eras, this has been maintained through narratives of myth, legend, religiously themed ordinances, rituals, and social hierarchies of power and their edicts. The thoughts, beliefs, and opinions that were 'available for use' within the social collective of the masses have always been limited by regulation. For such a long time, information came from localised sources, and as such were heavily governed by those same sources. Until very recently, information was spread slowly and passed on through linear transmission. By and large, outside of specific knowledge groupings and initiatory societies, the general state of social knowledge was extremely limited and relatively low level. States of consciousness were accessed by individuals unknowingly and sparsely; that is, upon a superficial level. Even today, those superficial levels exist, although not so widespread as in previous epochs. The point to make here is that as the general social expression of consciousness rises, so too do the control systems become more complex and sophisticated. Not only do such conditioning mechanisms operate through well-known social-cultural institutions—such as education, law and order, the media, and many more (as have been well documented)—they also operate more stealthily as, for example, through paranormal phenomena, as this chapter explores. As paranormal investigator Jacques Vallee stated:

> I propose the hypothesis that there is a control system for human consciousness … Human life is ruled by imagination and myth. These obey strict laws and they, too, are governed by control systems … What could paranormal phenomena control? I suggest that it is human belief that is being controlled and conditioned.[1]

What is suggested here is that the human belief system is a flexible playing field that has been experimented with. Over a long period of time, people have had their limits tested to accept previously unimagined ideas. Various and new mythologies are formed and planted into mass human consciousness. The most common response from the individual is to fit analogous data into pre-existing parameters of thought that then form 'reality boxes' in an attempt to stave off the invasion of the irrational or unknown. When the irrational and/or unknown encroaches upon one's consensus reality, a person is forced to 'close up' or change at a personal level to re-adapt—which is the easiest? A variety of tactics and influences exist within our general range of perceptions to control human beliefs, ideas, and ideals (that then form our ideologies). These modulating factors then gain a controlling influence over the relationship between human consciousness and physical reality. Such mechanisms have been in force throughout a great span of human history and have operated to manipulate human minds by sources unknown and largely external to us. These are deliberate attempts to diminish our sense of reality, and from this to make people more suggestible and open for programming, and also to create a psychic numbness that restricts the range of human perception. In more recent times, such programming has been applied to what is termed paranormal, metaphysical, and spiritual phenomena and experience.

Socio-spiritual engineering

Socio-spiritual engineering can be regarded as a form of 'culture-making' that has been prevalent throughout many cultural events and iconic movements. Some of these strategies were developed and implemented through high-level institutes that establish themselves as credible social enterprises.[2] The structures that uphold physical reality (including belief structures) are being diametrically positioned against any phenomena that may substantiate a spiritual or metaphysical reality. In order to draw conscious attention away from interest or alignment with aspects of the metaphysical realm, strategies within the lesser 'inverted' reality are established that create a fragmentation. That is, the tangibility of the physical domain, and the intangibility of the metaphysical realm, are not only placed in opposition but their potentials are fragmented. It has become a known method that phenomena and events are orchestrated that serve to break down the wholeness or credibility of each realm. And in this, the 'unidentified spectre' plays the perfect role. Mysterious or so-called unexplained phenomena act as a direct challenge to the consensus reality that is conditioned into our diverse societies. As writer Jasun Horsley puts it: 'Reality itself is the result of Consensus, and Consensus is merely an unconscious kind of conspiracy'.[3] The conspiracy is widespread and becomes the greatest club that almost everyone is a part of. They join the gang, accept the rules (the main narrative), and abide by the agreed ideology (dominant perspectives/perceptions). Consensus reality is, as Horsley rightly says, the ultimate secret society and most people are not even aware of its existence, or that they have been inducted as members. A stable consensus reality also establishes a stable collective mind; and stable minds are harder to reshape into new reality boxes should an alternative arise. The old adage was that if you wanted to introduce a new idea into a group/community, you first had to wait for the older minds (or olderminded people) to die out. Certain tweaks could be introduced intergenerationally, yet these were long-term projects. To have a collective mindset within the lesser reality that is more susceptible to rapid programming and psychological fluctuations, it is best to maintain a series of 'anomalies' within the system that can be utilised to create episodes of fragmentation and disassociation. And these are when spectres are brought out from behind the veil.

Mystification has long been a highly effective weapon of psychological warfare. Such elements have also played into the creation of myths as a form of social engineering. Social myths and mystification can be used as channels for the directing of, and influence of, the human psyche and psychic energies. Manipulated and/or controlled events have the power to affect and influence both the conscious and the unconscious mind. This can be utilised to create a split between what we are told to believe through our conditioning and what may be experienced in the metaphysical realm. This discrepancy can serve to create a rift in the human psyche and to fragment our reality boxes. This may result in greater bouts of irrationality and sow the seeds of psychological imbalance. Paranormal phenomena can be utilised to create an ambiguity that then produces a state of 'deferred closure'. That is, because the conditioned rational mind cannot create a closure (i.e. there is no ultimate solution), this creates a dissonance. This dissonance is further reinforced through the dissemination and circulation of many alternative answers that whilst promising to satisfy, instead end up confusing the human mind by not allowing it to find a consistent view of reality.

This produces a state of 'closure-starvation' that is likely to persuade a person to accept the next explanation that offers some closure relief. It is a procedure of mind programming and manipulation that is increasingly common within inverted reality. General mind programming and conditioning operate through established institutions such as education, politics, the media, etc; whereas the medium of psycho-spiritual phenomena allows conditioning to be implanted more deeply and directly for it bypasses much of the conscious mind. This way, methods of psychological splintering and trauma can be utilised, as I shall come to later. The fact that such implanting can occur with relatively no knowledge or awareness of it shows how little we know about the psychic world of the human being.

Over the last century—and especially since the middle of the 20th century—there has been a significant shift in people's belief patterning regarding the concept of the invisible and the unknown. These shifts have been occurring outside of recognised and established social structures, which gives them their potency. We may ask the question: what could be the control target for psycho-spiritual (aka paranormal) phenomena? The most likely answer is human belief systems. The external layering of the dominant reality consensus works upon the meta-logical level, and this seeks to programme the conscious mind of the individual as well as the collective. Yet the subconscious (collective) mind is influenced more upon the metaphysical level—as was well known to Carl Jung. And in this space, many of our mythological structures have been changing and/or reprogrammed. Into this space has seen the arrival of a variation of psychic phenomena and experiences. The human collective consciousness has been experiencing bouts of cosmism and trauma almost side by side. And what may be at stake here within this struggle for the subconscious mind is the very concept of our humanity. It is not simply our notions of human freedom that are in danger here but the understanding and experience of our *Beingness*.

In these modern times, humanity is experiencing a form of existential crisis that can be framed as a *psychic crisis*. At the same time, the solution lies where it has always been: within ourselves. The contours of the lesser reality are shifting; so too will the expression of the human subconscious as it manifests in world events. As Jung noted later in his life: 'Coming generations will have to take account of this momentous transformation if humanity is not to destroy itself through the might of its own technology and science'.[4] The metaphysical backdrop of the world informs the meta-logical front stage. Life experience in the lesser reality—the Inversion—is based on ritual. This is evident when we come to understand that ritual is the intentional design and correspondence of symbols, words, and coordinated actions. It is ceremonial action performed according to a prescribed order. And what do we see in the everyday world around us? We see organised routines, ceremonies, sacrificial events (wars), symbolism, advertising, slogans, and all the rest. Humanity, for the most part, is immersed within a medium of ritual. And rituals are manipulated practices to obtain a prescribed outcome. Increasingly so, the spectres and spooks of our ritualistic environment are manifesting—and they are more than just bursts of ectoplasm. The dreaming mind, in which humanity is enmeshed, has long been co-opted for the manipulation of awareness and the control of perception. This is the utilisation of ritual for the darker aspects of magic—the art of subterfuge and deception. The dreaming mind is not a false one, for it responds to those who know how best to engage and participate within it. It all depends on who has the upper hand. It is not so much a false reality rather than an alternative one. As it is said in the gnostic Gospel of Thomas: 'Whoever has come to understand the world has found only a corpse, and whoever has found a corpse is superior to the world'. Here, we may read that 'corpse' can also refer to the outer shell—the 'dead skin'. When we come to a deeper perception of the nature of our world (the lesser reality), we see the outer layering, the dead skin, that forms the rituals of this world. And those who are able to perceive this are 'superior to the world' in this knowing. And yet it is this very degree of knowing which is being constantly lulled to sleep by the coercive lullabies of the inverted 'dreaming' realm.

Socio-spiritual engineering targets the collective mind, and thus the individual mind, through manipulating and influencing the perceptions of how people view their world. These forces of influence operate both externally and internally as their medium is the transmission of information that many people receive through thinking patterns. It becomes increasingly difficult to distinguish between the imaginary, the deception, the quasi-reality, and the lesser reality, as people's reality-tunnels are continuously manipulated. Without most people's awareness, fragmentation and splintering of the human psyche is in effect. Whilst this is occurring, other elements within the dreaming mind can go ahead without our knowing—just as a magician uses the white rabbit to distract our attention from the source of the trickery. The result is that what is perceived as 'an all-inclusive reality' that becomes our realm of existence is actually a controlled environment that is anything but all-inclusive. Rather, it is fragmented and stitched together through narratives, stories, and conditioning programmes. Thus, the Inversion is a heavily manipulated environment where 'psychic-hacking', through ritual and cultural engineered events, exerts a metaphysical uncertainty and imbalance within many unsuspecting people.

There are some critical observers who regard the UFO phenomena of the last 70 years or so as also playing into the manipulations of global mind programming. As Jasun Horsley writes:

> through creating quasi-fictional memories of alien abduction (with the cooperation of Hollywood, network TV shows, UFO researchers and authors, experiencers speaking publicly about their experiences, et al.), these individual distortions of reality were then able to enter into the collective experience ...[5]

Paranormal phenomena allows the more transcendental part of the human psyche, says Horsley, to intervene and 'rescue' us from mundane reality by 'abducting' us into its realm. And this realm is real enough, albeit it is a dissociated one. In this way, certain paranormal and/or psycho-spiritual encounters and experiences—whether 'real' or not—may serve as a form of initiation into a type of social trauma. It is a trauma that acts on a subtle level, integrating itself into the socio-cultural psyche in a way that splinters the wholeness of the collective psyche without pushing it beyond the bounds of social functionality. In this way, UFO encounters and alien abduction experiences 'may be a way for some of us to allow such traumatic material into our awareness in a more "magical" (transcendental) guise'.[6] Voices of authority, such as national governments, have been heavily involved in the manipulation of how psychic phenomena are presented to the public; especially so regarding the matter of UFOs. For their part, they have been officially denying their existence whilst at the same time covertly leaking stories confirming that UFOs *do* exist. This form of 'subliminal contradiction technique' has been massively increased in recent years as many top-level sources, including the Pentagon, have gone on record to disclose UFO activity.[7] Further, in what can be seen as another form of cognitive programming, the United States authorities have begun to refer to UFO phenomena as Unidentified Aerial Phenomena (UAP). These forms of incessant denial followed by bouts of official or 'officially leaked' disclosure and recognition creates a subconscious contradiction that goes towards fixing an extreme form of *cognitive dissonance* within the public mindset. This ongoing inconsistency between two beliefs does not create a resolution but rather solidifies the uncertainty and dissonance through these well-placed subliminal contradictions. When a subliminal contradiction is accepted into the individual and collective perception without initial resistance, then the critical faculty is deactivated which leaves the mind vulnerable and receptive to suggestion. If, at any point in this saga, an official admission appears claiming to give the 'official version' of UFO events, then the general public are more likely to accept it, and perhaps with relief and gratitude that an answer has finally been found. Yet this relief comes as a 'resolution response' within the mind programming. Here, UFO phenomena are being slyly blended with psychic, paranormal, and metaphysical aspects as a way to colonise and reprogramme the 'spiritual' domain. These are cunning manoeuvres within the Inversion, for many people (in Westernised modernity especially) tend to confuse psychic experience with spiritual attainment. The tendency to willingly indulge in certain psychic or paranormal experiences may work to strengthen the false programming rather than strengthening the inner self.

There is a great need, and/or longing, within the human condition to access the non-visible realms; to access transcendental states that many infer bring them closer to a sense of Origin or Source. This longing can be a weakness as much as a strength if a person is not able to show discernment. Belief and imagination can easily be flipped into ideology, opinion, and fantasy. The corridor between realities is, in a genuine sense, based on the beliefs that programme our minds. And it is human belief that allows interventions and unidentified spectres into our realm. The question that needs to be asked is: is humanity being engineered and programmed into allowing these interventions? Each emergence and/or intervention requires our belief in it if it wishes to stay here for longer than a brief moment. Within the dreaming mind, *potentialities* become realities through an acknowledgement and then through belief systems—even if such acknowledgement is only quasi, such as in uncertain disbelief. The greater the sense of disbelief, the greater the insecurity and doubt, the easier it is to apply external programmes to people's minds. In recent years especially, there has been a dramatic rise in insecurity alongside paranormal and psycho-spiritual activity.

This is the perfect recipe for splintering the collective psyche and exercising subtle programmes of conscious and unconscious trauma.

A traumatised reality

The everyday world has its full dosage of depression, anxiety issues, and suicides. There has long been a malaise simmering within the undercurrents of the life experience. Modern societies seem to expect a psychological reorganisation of the social system, every now and again. It acts as a form of recalibration to the fluctuating contours of the collective dreaming mind. Within these contours, crisis and trauma are not so much isolated events but currents within the continual process that keeps the social realm from settling down to a comfortable bed. Whether we are aware of it or not, trauma has always been incorporated into the 'norm' in human society; from medical birthing procedures, random acts of violence, institutionalised madness, authoritarian fear strategies, population indoctrinations, religious-cult programming, conditioned education, and more (as explored in the previous chapter). All these elements combine to create variations upon a divided consciousness. Carl Jung referred to this state as *dissociation* and it acts as a polarising force against psychic integration. Philosopher Charles Upton believes that modernity has led people to a 'nihilistic worship of fragmentation and chaos' that masquerades as cultural diversity.[8] The human psyche is already fragile and hence vulnerable to further triggers to dissociation. These triggers, it is suggested, have been arriving through paranormal experiences; the top of the list being the 'extra-terrestrial issue' and the UFO phenomena. This is significant given that in recent months, beginning in 2020, there has been a heightened presence of UFO-related material within the mainstream media. Normally a subject of mainstream ridicule or avoidance, major news outlets (in the US especially) have been carrying reports over 'credible' verified sightings where once this subject was deliberately avoided. There is speculation that this sudden rise in mainstream reporting (orchestrated through the intelligence agencies) belongs to an engineered propaganda operation for preparing the collective mindset for a new paranormal narrative. That is, another reality-tunnel is being constructed for mass release. For a long time, the subject of aliens belonged to a historical lineage of phenomena that included fairies, little people, nature spirits, djinns, demons, etc. Jungian psychoanalyst Donald Kalsched notes that the word 'daimonic' comes from *daiomai*, which means to divide, and that it originally referred to moments of divided consciousness. Kalsched has studied trauma in relation to mytho-poetic manifestations and psycho-spiritual development. Triggers from the mytho-spiritual realm, which includes paranormal experience, can cause a fragmentation of the consciousness—especially in less-grounded individuals. In this case, the external event fuses with a person's inner psychological state. As Kalsched notes: 'The full pathological effect of trauma requires an outer event *and a psychological factor*. Outer trauma alone doesn't split the psyche. *An inner psychological agency—occasioned by the trauma—does the splitting'.*[9] Jung referred to these states as 'splinter-psyches' where one of the splinter complexes, after the initial trauma, attempts to protect the regressed part like a guardian. This may result in preventing any further *psychic integration* as the experience cannot be fully integrated or processed by the psyche. The person may try to re-enact or regain the traumatic experience as a way of gaining closure. This may explain some of the obsessive behaviour of paranormal experiencers after the event to keep searching for repeat experiences.

This same behaviour can also be applied to what is termed as a spiritual phenomenon. The modern world is awash with 'spiritual retreats' of one form or another. The marketplace for 'spiritual paths' is also regularly full of clients. The danger here is that some of these paths may lead not further inward toward an integrated psychological state but rather further into dissociated states as a form of escapism. As Jasun Horsley notes:

> Bliss states might *appear* to be leading to fuller embodiment when they are really the result of the mind using spiritual fantasies (dissociation) to release anesthetizing chemicals in the body *to stave off integration* (just as heroin or morphine can be used to create pleasing physical sensations) … This is a very apparent danger of 'spiritual awakenings' that result from trauma.[10]

There can be scaled levels of 'awakenings' within the dreaming mind, as brilliantly shown by Christopher Nolan's film *Inception* (2010). In this filmic scenario, ideas are implanted into a person's subconscious at various levels within the dream-state. Within each dream level, the person 'believes' they are awake and thus do not perceive the manipulations and programming. It is only by having their conscious awareness triggered that can they break from the subconscious programming. This is an excellent analogy for what is occurring within the various states of the *waking dream* of the Inversion. The waking dream-state is particularly deceptive for our minds are convinced that we are awake and thus not dreaming nor susceptible to programming. And yet the human subconscious is being programmed constantly—if not, there would be no success through propaganda and advertising.

The devious agenda of psycho-spiritual programming through metaphysical events is that the implants bypass the conscious mind almost immediately and attach themselves to the parts of the subconscious. That is, the programming bypasses the usual gatekeepers to our minds. Once these mechanisms are in place, then they can be activated whenever there is a need to trigger a part of the collective psyche. The UFO phenomenon has been gradually sown into our cultural soils for the past seven or eight decades at least. At the same time, there has been the seeds of trauma scattered throughout various extra-terrestrial contact experiences. Charles Upton regards the alien question as a form of programming to mimic spiritual realities on the psycho-physical level, and so prepare the way for something even more traumatic. Other commentators, such as the well-respected Harvard psychiatrist John E. Mack, recognised that ET experiencers appeared to undergo a psychic triggering that activated their sense of evolutionary development. The cosmic bubble within the lesser reality (the Inversion) has begun to tear, and through these rips are appearing the unidentified spectres of uncertain purpose. The French mystic-philosopher Rene Guenon wrote several books warning that increased materialism and physical trappings will lead to a 'solidification of the world' resulting in 'fissures' opening up through which 'infra-psychic' forces can enter.[11] These forces, amongst others, are all impacting the human psychosphere and rewiring our internal programming.

There may certainly be some physical brain rewiring going on. As infamous UFO contactee Whitley Streiber says: 'If you actually wanted people to increase the use of the right brain, then stressing them would be a way to do it. If you apply trauma in the right way, what you are actually doing is reengineering the brain'[12] The spectres and spooks of the Inversion may represent equally an expansion of consciousness as well as a vehicle for traumatic brain programming. Jasun Horsley

questions whether splitting the human psyche could be a way of allowing, or letting through, certain 'hostile forces' that may be a part of the
shadow psyche. These shadows might then be materialised, or at least
experienced, by the psyche as material phenomena. Horsley goes on
to say:

> Intelligence black ops that simulate alien abduction—just as
> Hollywood dramatizations do on a more open and wide-scale
> level—may be a way to shape and direct the narrative in order to
> control the ways in which we experience these fragmentary psychic
> forces.[13]

Letting through these unidentified spectres may be just some of the
programmes within the lesser reality to splinter the collective human
psyche and steer it further away from psychic integration and wholeness. This agenda relates to 'reality hacking' or a hijacking of reality, as
I explored in an earlier book.[14]

Interestingly, much of metaphysical phenomena are classed as part
of the 'new paradigm' and suchlike, as if these elements are part of a
new reality consciousness. And yet the very notion of paradigms—and
hence, the concept of a 'new paradigm'—is an alternative emergence
from within the existing structures. As such, metaphysical phenomena
and experiences may serve to deceive if they are utilised for simply rear-
ranging the pre-existing furniture of our minds rather than breaking
out of these programmed reality boxes. Dreaming within the waking
dream has many levels, and things are just not what they seem. To shift
from one part of the dreaming—within the Inversion—may only represent a slip from one aspect of the dream-matrix into another. And this
deception causes people to believe it is a 'new reality' when in fact it is
another layer within the multi-faceted 'matrix onion'. Another aspect to
consider is that metaphysical experiences tend to take the experiencer
away from their bodily presence. As the metaphysical and paranormal
threads become increasingly woven into the mainstream narrative,
we may be witnessing a new reality-tunnel unfolding that requires a
subconscious rejection of the body. Is the controlling programme of
the Inversion now intent on moving toward a rejection of the bodily-
physical as part of the rising human-machine narrative? Does humanity
in this realm have a bodily future? These are some of the issues that will
be explored in the following chapters.

Notes

1. Jacques Vallee, *The Invisible College: What a Group of Scientists Has Discovered About UFO Influences on the Human Race* (Charlottesville: Anomalist Books, 2015), 199.
2. For example, in the UK, the Tavistock Institute.
3. Jasun Horsley, (aka Aeolus Kephas), *The Lucid View: Investigations into Occultism, Ufology, and Paranoid Awareness* (Illinois: Adventures Unlimited, 2004), 59.
4. C. G. Jung, *The Undiscovered Self (with Symbols and The Interpretation of Dreams)* (Princeton: Princeton University Press, 2010), 60.
5. Jasun Horsley, *Prisoner of Infinity: UFOs, Social Engineering, and the Psychology of Fragmentation* (London: Aeon Books, 2018), 224.
6. Jasun Horsley, *Prisoner of Infinity: UFOs, Social Engineering, and the Psychology of Fragmentation* (London: Aeon Books, 2018), 135.
7. The public disclosure from governmental sources increased suddenly in 2021.
8. Charles Upton, *The Alien Disclosure Deception: The Metaphysics of Social Engineering* (Sophia Perennis, 2021).
9. Donald Kalsched, *The Inner World of Trauma: Archetypal Defences of the Personal Spirit* (London: Routledge, 1996), 14.
10. Jasun Horsley, *Prisoner of Infinity: UFOs, Social Engineering, and the Psychology of Fragmentation* (London: Aeon Books, 2018), 34.
11. See Guenon's *The Crisis of the Modern World*, and *The Reign of Quantity and the Signs of the Times.*
12. Cited in Jasun Horsley, *Prisoner of Infinity: UFOs, Social Engineering, and the Psychology of Fragmentation* (London: Aeon Books, 2018), 104.
13. Jasun Horsley, *Prisoner of Infinity: UFOs, Social Engineering, and the Psychology of Fragmentation* (London: Aeon Books, 2018), 223.
14. See *Hijacking Reality: The Reprogramming & Reorganization of Human Life* (2021).

CHAPTER 6

In thy body do I dwell
(the physical construct as host)

The Suns Light when he unfolds it. Depends on the Organ that
beholds it.

—William Blake

The body is coming back into sight as a site for experimentation and as
a target for a type of quasi-transcendence. In the Inversion, the physical
body has always been recognised as the vehicle through which life is
experienced. In other words, it is our *avatar* whilst in this realm. As such,
it has always been a site of contestation. In some religious circles, the
body is seen as a material distraction from the divine; as such, its influence was seen as needing to be repressed and subjugated (which may
include certain physical deprivations, including self-harm). Various
religio-spiritual perspectives have regarded the physical body as an
obstacle, a barrier, to a sense of the sacred. The other extreme is that the
body is regarded as the ideal vehicle for experiencing the sensual and
sensuous—it is a vessel for indulgence and decadent experience. Still,
there has been no consensus reached over how to regard the vehicle
of the human physical body. In my earlier book—*Hijacking Reality*—I
noted how recent narratives are trying to place the human body as a
site of weakness. That is, the body is open and vulnerable to disease

and infection; it succumbs to ageing and exhaustion; it disallows the human being from the full range of experiences. In this light, narratives of transhumanism are attempting to gain ground as a way of offering an alternative to the 'weak body'. These, as I discussed previously, are attempts to drive the human experience deeper into materialism and a technocratic agenda for a digital-hybridisation programme within our societies.

The Inversion is steering ever forward into deeper and deeper realms of materialism. It is a narrative of quasi-transcendence through embedding deeper into the myth of technological salvation. The lines are not so much being drawn but being blurred. American writer Philip K. Dick, famous for his science fiction books that question the nature and validity of reality, spoke about the blurring of boundaries between body and environment in his 1972 speech 'The Android and the Human':

> Our environment, and I mean our man-made world of machines, artificial constructs, computers, electronic systems, interlinking homeostatic components—all of this is in fact beginning more and more to possess what the earnest psychologists fear the primitive sees in his environment: animation. In a very real sense our environment is becoming alive, or at least quasi-alive, and in ways specifically and fundamentally analogous to ourselves.[1]

This quasi-aliveness of the environment that Dick speaks about is the animating stage where relations between the human body and the Inversion begin to blur (and merge). As the sciences of the quantum have demonstrated, the subject–object world of *us-and-it* is an illusion. All materiality is in fact enmeshed within a quantum entangled energy matrix—and our bodies are somatically communicating with this energetic construct continuously. Much of Western spiritual-mystical practice is interpreted as a somatically-felt experience. The body is the instrument that receives and grounds the experience, whether it be in terms of the 'great flash', 'illuminating light', or the 'bodily rush'. The body is the human instrument for receiving, transforming, and sometimes transferring, energies. There are many 'bodies' in spiritual-mystic traditions, including the etheric, the astral, the ecstatic, the subtle, the higher, and others; the physical, material body is recognised as the densest of them all. Also, it is the 'easy target' since it resides fully within the material world and is open to social engineering and influence.

As cultural historian Morris Berman has noted, the body in history has always been a site of focus. It has helped define the experience of self/other and the outer/inner and has been regarded as the material vessel for the spiritual impulse.[2] Perhaps for this reason, many societies around the world have, at one time or another, attempted to suppress the power and expression of the human body. It could be that the controlling agencies within the Inversion regard the balanced, correctly functioning human body as a portal for infiltrating and navigating the perceptive wavelengths of reality. Many of the mystical traditions placed a strong emphasis on the purification of the human body; on it being free from toxins and corruptive influences. In this way, the physical vessel was said to receive the 'illuminations', or the 'mercy' of the sacred, divine impulse. The body acts as an antenna for the nourishing inspirations/energies of the soul. What better way to block these illuminations than to corrupt the body's purity through a polluting environment—socially, psychologically, and biologically? As such, the body has always been a site for the convergence of power and control. This body-power relationship has been a major theme in the work of French philosopher Michel Foucault. Foucault has deconstructed, in his critical history of modernity, how the body has been fought over as a site of power.[3] The physical body is also regarded as a location of resistance against the establishment powers. It is a fixed place where an individual can be located, found, and held accountable. And now that our physical movements are continually tracked through the digital infosphere, there is even less chance to escape the eye of authoritative surveillance. If we cannot escape from our bodies then, it would appear, we are forever within the system.

The human body has always been accepted as a unit within the social matrix. This has also been expanded to define bodies in terms of social institutions: we have the body politic, the social body, the scientific body, the medical body, the body of an organisation, etc. The once sacred site of the body, which was the vessel for somatic spiritual experiences, has been adopted, or co-opted, into a social construction of bodies that belong under control and subjugation of external authorities. In Gnostic terms, the body's site of power has been referred to as those of the 'sleepers' and the 'wakers'. Sleepers are those whose inner self has yet to break through the layers of the body's social conditioning. The somatic spiritual experience has been seen as a threat to hierarchical societies because it exists beyond their bounds of power. This is one reason why ecstatic experiences, whether through spiritual or other means, have been suppressed, outlawed, and discredited by orthodox religions and mainstream institutions alike. Ecstatic experiences that can break down the thinking patterns and conditioning structures of the Inversion are alarming for institutions of socio-political power. How can you control, regulate, and discipline a body, energy, or experience that has no physical location? Such intangible forces, such as the power of baraka, are positively infectious and beyond bounds.[4] As Berman notes:

> The goal of the Church (any church) is to obtain a monopoly on this vibratory experience, to channel it into its own symbol system, when the truth is that the somatic response is not the exclusive property of any given religious leader or particular set of symbols.[5]

In recent times, there has been an increasing focus on what is termed the innate consciousness of the body, and which has been revealed through such techniques as muscle testing. It is innate because it is inborn (born in and *of* the body), and it is instinctual. Somatic consciousness then is another word for our intuitive intelligence. It is an intelligence that can be communicated through the body, and it is this which threatens those that seek to control the dreaming mind of humanity. However, the matrix of reality is not a clean-cut realm.

We exist in an anthropological environment where nature and culture cannot be neatly divided. The physical realm is a fusion of the real/imagined, and where subject/object is blurred. Yet now, this hybridity is being further enforced and coalesced through genetic engineering, implants, augmented reality, and the sciences of nanotechnology, biotechnology, and information technology (including artificial intelligence). The Inversion is attempting to gain our willing compliance through offering a form of transcendence that goes *beyond* the body and the bodily senses.

The galactic gaze

The dreaming mind has always been tempted and awed by the stars beyond. There is perhaps no living person who has not gazed up into the night firmament and wondered about the cosmos *out there*. And perhaps, there have been those persons who upon gazing up wondered whether they were not living within some kind of bubble.

The dreamer's world has often been depicted as a bubble reality, most notably by the Renaissance alchemists, as later shown by this well-known engraving (Figure 1):

Figure 1 'The Alchemist's Gaze' (print of the Flammarion wood engraving, 1888)

The Philosopher's Stone lies outside of the realm of the Inversion; it can only be grasped by one who has exited from the dreamer's reality bubble (or perceptual prison). For most people, the spiralling star tapestry of the cosmos is the first step of the beyond. Reason enough, then, for this to have become the new destination for the modern pioneers within the lesser reality.

The break from the body begins at an early age through social conditioning. To some extent, all individuals have to relinquish some of the contact they have with the innate intelligence of the body (including the body of the natural world) by being incorporated into the 'social body'. And as the social body becomes increasingly enmeshed within the digitised landscape, this alienation from the body will only likewise increase. As touched upon in the previous chapter, the labyrinth of the pseudo-spiritual maze, along with paranormal experiences, also contributes to a form of 'bliss out' and further dissociation from body awareness. Modern culture's love affair with decadence, and the rise of sexualisation and drug indulgence, all contribute to a desensitisation of the body—even when the body is the medium of experience, such as in sexual experiences. As noted, this is a targeting of the 'pure body' so as to corrupt its potential for deciphering deeper layers within the Inversion. The body-medium for the life experience is also viewed by transhumanists as a hindrance to the evolutionary journey toward an 'immortal society' that is destined for the stars. This view is more keenly taken by mostly Western and 'elite' types who have begun to feed themselves upon a modern cosmic-religious mythic consciousness. This is what Jasun Horsley refers to as a 'Galactic religion', which seeks transcendence/ascension by leaving the planet and colonising others. It is a 'rich geek' religion based on accelerating technologies and pushed by the major tech-titan companies. As Horsley notes, rather than ascension, it is the reverse:

> It has to do with dissociation, the attempt of the traumatized psyche to split off from the body and float off into fantasy land, beyond the reach of reality and all the pain it entails. Bodies frozen on ice, souls lost in space, free, free from the terrible travails of the body.[6]

In such contexts as these, and more, there is a trauma being experienced through the physical body. Trauma can be related to dysfunctional energy being trapped within the body, causing discomfort and disease. In an attempt to escape the body of the planet, we are being forced to 'techno-transcend' the limitations of the biological human body. To travel into the stars, we are told, requires us to upload our consciousness into machinic devices and/or ethereal cloudscapes. In a bid to escape the confines of a depleting 'prison planet' we are being asked to put our faith—and our consciousness—into a new techno-prison. Yet who shall be the new guards? This could entail the trauma of a new birth—re-enacting the prongs of the biological birth passage yet through entry into yet another realm of the Inversion. There seems to be no genuine exit of the dreaming mind through consciousness upload—only a leap into another programmable maze, yet this time perhaps with less benevolent programmers.

In the Western psyche, there appears to be an ongoing splintering between 'inner-space' exploration and 'outer-space' exploration. The techno-dream of space colonisation is the new favoured trend whilst the inner-space research of the psyche is promoted as a dangerous and trickster landscape. *Outer space* is the new undiscovered realm that offers hope against the twilight of the body (including the body of the Earth). And yet such 'Galactic pioneers' seem driven less by a unified perception and more by forces arising within their splintered psyches that they have failed to integrate. These are the subconscious forces that grasp at survival, at any cost, and would willingly walk over the bodies of others to secure their own survival. Leaving the planetary body is only for the lucky few, whilst the rest must remain grounded—or with their minds in cloudscape orbit. *The trick of the Inversion is that there are endless doors to keep walking through, yet no exit to awaken out of.* By walking out of one dreamworld into another we may think we are free, yet we remain imprisoned within the dream still. Or worse, we unknowingly become our very own prison guards. There is the joke that goes: if god is so wise then why did he make humans out of meat?

No rockets will ever create enough thrust to take us where we truly need to go, for awakening from the gravity of the Inversion is an *inner-space* journey. It is the colonising of the quiet kind—of ourselves. By striving to attain the orbital Overview Effect we are missing the real point, which is the 'Inner view' from within ourselves.

The body as the holy host

The Inversion is unsure of what to make of the human physical body. Is it our saviour—our holy host?—or a danger to our own progress and a threat to the agenda of others? As I have written previously, the narratives of a new biopower have brought to the fore a medical-political establishment within many of our societies worldwide. The biology of control is now a major player within the current realm of lived experience. There is now a noticeable rush to gain a political-corporate control over the access, use, and sovereignty of the human body. In a very real sense, it is the individual's last line of physical defence. Each individual is a conscious entity (a spiritual essence) that is operating within this material realm through the vehicle of the physical body. As such, we are uniting with a biological partner. We are a merged being: as it is said, a union of flesh and spirit. Whilst the spirit—the essential being—is immortal, it has to abide by the biological limitations of the physical host. Because of this crucial fact, external control agendas are determined to not only gain power over the outer aspects of the body (its freedoms, utility, mobility, etc.) but also, via interventions, to have control over its internal functioning (DNA code, intra-communication, and more).

The human body functions upon many varied levels and acts as many things—including as a receiver, filter, and transmitter of energies and information. It is only the false, manipulated narrative that posits the human body as a 'biohazard'. By using this designation, external agencies of authority can seek to further contain and control the movement of the body as well as gaining internal access through chemical and pharmaceutical interventions. These possibilities were foreseen by many, not least by the social philosopher (and possible predictive programmer) Aldous Huxley. Even as far back as the 1950s, Huxley envisaged the encroachment of scientism to gain increasing intervention into the human body:

> Meanwhile pharmacology, biochemistry and neurology are on the march, and we can be quite certain that, in the course of the next few years, new and better chemical methods for increasing suggestibility and lowering psychological resistance will be discovered. Like everything else, these discoveries may be used well or badly. They may help the psychiatrist in his battle against mental illness, or they may help the dictator in his battle against freedom.[7]

And yet, this is still a viewpoint based on the material and physical sciences. It does not represent a deeper, spiritual perspective. This was to be provided by the Austrian philosopher and proponent of spiritual science, Rudolf Steiner. In talks given during September–October 1917, Steiner had the presence of vision to discuss the later potential interventions and influence over the human body. He said that:

> Taking a 'sound point of view', people will invent a vaccine to influence the organism as early as possible, preferably as soon as it is born, so that this human body never even gets the idea that there is a soul and a spirit.[8]

Clearly, this shows that the human physical body is a site of target in an attempt to kerb or block reception of spiritual forces. Through what may appear to be a 'sound point of view', a range of socio-cultural narratives will be created and propagated, according to Steiner, that will push an agenda of increased medical intervention. And these medically backed ideas have the aim 'to find a vaccine that will drive all inclination towards spirituality out of people's souls when they are still very young, and this will happen in a roundabout way through the living body'.[9] Humanity has arrived at that time now, if we observe current events and their related consequences. We are now at a time within the 21st century where we are witnessing the transmutation of living beings—and bodies. The human being has arrived at a threshold previously unknown to it, and there are forces compelling the human to step over and through it. It is a threshold that will recode environments and bodies. The threshold is the point where a genetic deterritorialisation process can begin, and from which we may witness the emergence of a new organism different from the current one. It is a threshold of recombination and recodification; a new assemblage that represents yet another phase within the Inversion. From here on, we are biologically vulnerable to an encroaching machinic impulse that, by its very nature, will morph bodily combinations into machinic connections.

Our bodies are reaching an exhaustion point. The crises we now face across the body of the Earth are from a collapse of the individual, social, and psychological body. Already, the social mind is in trauma, and the body is showing this illness or dis-ease. The Inversion has made sure that the biological and psychological dimension has coalesced. The ripple of a bodily trauma is being felt across the planetary membrane as people are forced to unnaturally detach from the physical world around them. New physical arrangements of dislocation (lockdowns) and social avoidance are becoming established practices within our societies. These unnatural ordinances are creating cognitive and bodily dissonance. Bio-traumas have arisen that are affecting our sensibilities. New bodily phobias have been set in motion. This is the newly inverted threshold; it is 'a threshold marked by low-intensity trauma, sub-acute depression and a sort of fogging in emotional attention'.[10] The threshold of deterritorialisation has enforced a changing perception of the body. We are sensing alterations in human bodily awareness and receptivity. There is a deprivation too. The body is being pulled back from its natural organic terrain. It is being made to retreat from physical presence and away from the reassuring touch. It is as if the body is being reconfigured to devolve away from the sensate and into a new digitally articulated environment. The aliveness is being substituted by decomposition and the fear of decay and deterioration.

In the modern age, death has replaced sex as the modern taboo. The sanitised environment of the hospital has replaced the home as the place for passing away. The experience of death and dying has become detached from community life with the effect that emotion and closeness has been replaced by medical management. The dying body has become inverted into a thing of disgust and embarrassment. Death has now become something shameful—a forbidden process. Death is a modern scandal. Modern life has internalised the rejection of death and we are coded to cringe at the thought of bodily deterioration. Death is a loser. To die is to lose, to fail. There is no room for failure within the deepening layers of machinic materialism and computational competition. Death can be replaced by tech-assisted immortality in the new posthuman future. Alternatively, the body can be transcended through transhumanism so that death no longer haunts the halls of the physical flesh. These are the new imaginings in the realm of machinic desire. Humanity is on the threshold of venturing into an Inversion of codified imagination and upturned desires. Desire has overtaken pleasure. It has become a form of cognitive-bodily pain-gratification. And it is the social sphere within the Inversion that creates and sustains this desirous torment and torture of the unattainable. And within the unattainable, greater forms of outer control must be endorsed to compensate. For this reasoning, current forces have begun to establish new paths of control over life processes. And this, by intent and not coincidence, aligns with the rise of the machinic impulse. The question that now needs to be asked—and which I shall address in Part II—is whether the machine impulse is evolutionary or devolutionary in terms of human life upon this planet.

Notes

1. Philip K. Dick, 'Cosmogeny and Cosmology', in The Shifting Realities of Philip K. Dick: Selected Literary and Philosophical Writings, ed. Lawrence Sutin (New York: Vintage Books, 1995), 183.
2. Morris Berman, Coming to Our Senses: Body and Spirit in the Hidden History of the West (New York: HarperCollins, 1990).
3. See especially Michel Foucault's Discipline and Punish.
4. Baraka, a prominent concept in Islamic mysticism, refers to a flow of grace and spiritual power that can be transmitted.

5. Morris Berman, *Coming to Our Senses: Body and Spirit in the Hidden History of the West* (New York: HarperCollins, 1990), 146.
6. Jasun Horsley, *Prisoner of Infinity: UFOs, Social Engineering, and the Psychology of Fragmentation* (London: Aeon Books, 2018), 189.
7. Aldous Huxley, *Brave New World Revisited* (London: Chatto & Windus, 1959), 107–108.
8. Rudolf Steiner, *The Fall of the Spirits of Darkness* (Forest Row: Rudolf Steiner Press, 2008), 85.
9. Rudolf Steiner, *The Fall of the Spirits of Darkness* (Forest Row: Rudolf Steiner Press, 2008), 199–200.
10. Franco Berardi, *The Third Unconscious* (London: Verso, 2021), 70.

PART II

THE MACHINIC IMPULSE

At each stage man has to abandon the secure, the trusted, and—
for his present moment—the ultimate. At each stage he has to
struggle with the denying force of inertia. He has to surmount a
mental obstacle as once he had to surmount biological obstacles.
If he succeeds, he learns more, understands more, gets closer
and closer to participating. It may be that he is now required
to confront—and accept—the mechanism of his own evolution.

—Ernest Scott, *The People of the Secret*

CHAPTER 7

The unreal machine: 1
(the struggle for human authenticity)

> There is a long-distance race on between humanity's technological
> capability, which is like a stallion galloping across the fields, and
> humanity's wisdom, which is more like a foal on unsteady legs.
> —Nick Bostrom

There could seemingly be good reason to credit the First and Second
Industrial Revolutions as the birthplace of the machinic impulse. Yet
this would be inaccurate. The history of humanity and technology,
however, goes far back into our deep past. Magic, science, alchemy, for
example, are also forms of technology as what technology represents is
a sphere of human-related activity that interacts with and transforms
substances and forces of the outer mineral world. Yet what I refer to
as the 'machinic impulse' is not the same thing as technology. It is not
a *thing*, a *structure* or even a *process*: it is a specific style of force, with
its own vibrational identity, and which aims to recalibrate, revise, and
recode human life *in its image* (energy state). It is a vibrational construct
that is also available to being managed and directed into intentional
pathways. Who, or what, would take control over such an energetic
impulse? We may gain some clues as we venture further in our travels

through the Inversion. Let us begin by observing some emergent sign-posts over the last 70 years.

In the second half of the 20th century there emerged the early waves that began the convergence of the body, spirit, and mind. One wave included the physical (bodily) research fields of cybernetics, computer programming, and early artificial intelligence. These are then interwoven with themes of the mind and spirit in psychedelic experimentation, mystical philosophies, transcendental movements, magical revivals, shamanism, and many other forms of transformational experimentation. The list of names that come up in these years is very, very long. As a brief incursion, it can be seen how the emergence of computer terminology gave rise to notions of programming—and metaprogramming—the human body as a biocomputer. This image was reinforced by Dr John C. Lilly's book *Programming and Metaprogramming in the Human Biocomputer*, which described some of his experiments on human consciousness and human-dolphin communication. Metaprogramming also became a core theme of the writings of Timothy Leary and Robert Anton Wilson, who produced such works as *Exo-Psychology: A Manual on the Use of the Human Nervous System According to the Instructions of the Manufacturers*, and *Prometheus Rising*, respectively. Both these works discuss an eight-circuit model of consciousness that is part of a path in neurological evolution. Both authors, Leary especially, took it upon themselves to evolve a philosophy stating that the future evolution of human civilisation is encoded in our DNA. They speculated that the human nervous system is already hardwired for evolutionary mutation.

Earlier in the 20th century saw the arrival of the ideas of Caucasian mystic G. I. Gurdjieff, who spoke of the human being in terms of a 'man-machine' that was asleep to life and could be triggered into wakeful activation. Leary, in Gurdjieffian overtones, would call for humanity to 'wake up, mutate, and ascend'.[1] Strange and unusual teachings began to emerge that suggested the next stage for humanity was for the species to actively epigenetically reprogramme its DNA through a fusion of transcendental and/or psychedelic practices. This modern Western melting pot saw the rise of similar motifs such as E. J. Gold's *The Human Biological Machine as a Transformational Apparatus*. Within the Inversion emerged a new playing field in the politics of experimentation involving the inner spaces of the human biological body and its extended mind field. This then became fertile ground for the computing trope of 'programming' and 'metaprogramming' to emerge and be hijacked to sow the seeds for the rise of the machinic impulse.

The rise of the modern-day robots literally happened after the Dartmouth Summer Research Project on Artificial Intelligence, in the summer of 1956, heralded the beginning of the field of AI. College campuses and defence departments suddenly accelerated their earnest journey along the research road that spawned the controversial concept of consciousness upload. One of the more vocal supporters of this 'mind-in-machine' notion was robotics researcher Hans Moravec. Moravec, whose books include *Mind Children* and *Robot*, outlined a future where the human mind can be uploaded as a precursor to full artificial intelligence. Similarly, cognitive scientist Marvin Minksy (who was one of the 1956 gang that announced the field of AI) espoused a philosophy that saw no fundamental difference between humans and machines, which he put forward in such works as *Society of Mind*. Artificial intelligence, it seems, is uncannily consistent with the Christian belief in resurrection and post-body immortality. Does this make AI research and the machinic impulse into a sacred enterprise? Historian of technology David F. Noble noted that the AI project is imbued with its own trajectory of transcendence:

> The thinking machine was not, then, an embodiment of what was specifically human, but of what was specifically divine about humans—the immortal mind … The immortal mind could evolve independently into ever higher forms of artificial life, reunited at last with its origin, the mind of God.[2]

This fertile ground soon sprouted several futurist movements and their manifestos that led to the establishment of transhumanism. It was not long before the transhumanist voices were declaring that the Technological Singularity is near.[3]

Yet there had been earlier voices within the inverted landscape that saw the signs of what was coming—or perhaps had been handed the blueprint for predictive programming. Some of these were writers of science fiction that found fiction the most suitable vehicle for sharing these future scenarios. Most notable amongst these were George Orwell (*Nineteen Eighty-Four*—1949) and Aldous Huxley (*Brave New World*—1932). In 1959, Aldous Huxley published *Brave New World Revisited* which contained his reflections on how far the 'inverted world' had come in realising his earlier fictional visions. Huxley had observed how the rise of *technique* was becoming a stealth part of our modern societies. The notion of 'technique' here implies a particular way or set of methods to achieve a goal, a desired outcome. Specifically, 'technique' was suggesting a mechanised arrangement or pattern of methods to achieve particular ends. The emergence of efficient and managed 'techniques' also allowed for the rise of the *machinic impulse* into human lives. And Huxley had spotted, quite early on, how political and high-end commercial interests were developing a range of techniques for manipulating the thoughts and feelings of the masses. Writing in the 1950s, Huxley stated that,

> We see, then, that modern technology has led to the concentration of economic and political power, and to the development of a society controlled (ruthlessly in the totalitarian states, politely and inconspicuously in the democracies) by Big Business and Big Government.[4]

In the years to come, Huxley envisioned that most of humanity would be facing the choice between anarchy and totalitarian control. Further, without their conscious knowing, most people would inevitably slip into a 'polite' form of totalitarianism where they would have the illusion of individuality whilst conforming to a social uniformity. This would echo Gurdjieff's insistence that the human being was an automation—a 'man-machine'—that could not act from its own volition. What is being covertly introduced through technologically managed techniques, observed Huxley, is the 'reduction of unmanageable multiplicity to comprehensible unity ... the practical reduction of human diversity to subhuman uniformity, of freedom to servitude'.[5] Such processes as these are transforming organic social communities and groupings into mechanical arrangements, and this is the machinic impulse carried within the current wave of technological change.

Social organisation is fast becoming instrumental rather than conscious and organic. Within this context, instrumental power is able to gain a dominant foothold, as I shall explain shortly. The power play within the Inversion is able to flip back to front how we consider human consciousness in a bid to more easily steer it toward a machinic version. The modern scientific narrative falsely states, and teaches, that consciousness arises as a consequence of the complexity of the human brain. This wholly, and deliberate, materialistic paradigm states that the software (consciousness) is an accidental by-product of how the hardware (brain) operates. This pattern of thinking then makes it easier to designate the human being as a 'product' of external stimuli; similar to how a robotic, mechanical being would form its behaviour from external, or programmed stimuli. There is an almost non-visible demarcation line between the mechanical being and the 'accidental human'. As Italian philosopher Franco Berardi puts it: 'Since the human being is the product (cultural, technical, historical) of countless influences, impulses, and implementations, we may infer that it is an android who wrongly believes itself to be a human'.[6] This inverted reality is slyly shifting dominance from consciousness to intellect. It is the machinic impulse that favours the intellect over high-vibrational consciousness. This could mark the crossover from genuine human individualism into a regulated and unified collectivism of the masses.

It is becoming rarer these days as we travel through the Inversion to come across a genuine 'individual'. The notion of the individual has been twisted into a modern form of the self-centred individual who strives to get ahead of others; this trait is now lauded in our societies as a hero figure, in the US especially. The modern faux individual within the unreal machine is a regulated and 'datafied' point within the collective mass. Human relationships are being replaced by machine processes, creating a vast digital apparatus for the next phase of the Inversion.

The machinic apparatus

> With this reorientation from knowledge to power, it is no longer enough to automate information flows *about us*; the goal now is to *automate us*.
>
> —Shoshana Zuboff

At all times we are compelled to adapt to our conditions of existence; that is, the conditions of the current state of the Inversion with which we inhabit. As these conditions change, we too are forced to adapt as part of the strategy. And here comes the point of contention, as some people feel the inner need to explore their self-development, which is the process of *individuation*. Yet there are opposing forces that seek to create managed social identities that correspond to the mass social body—these are the forces of *managed individualisation*. The person has an individual social identity, yet it is in conformity with the social collective. Furthermore, this social identity is now in the process of being passed along to the management of the machinic architecture. Less and less is our behaviour in this reality being shaped by social forces; and more and more are we being tweaked into behavioural traits preferable to the machinic impulse. The shift is into a mode whereby a surrounding architecture of monitoring and surveillance will aspire to modify real-time actions in the 'real world'. Is humanity on the road to becoming yet another device within an overarching architecture of automation?

The term the technologists use for ways to structure and direct action to elicit a desired behaviour or outcome is *choice architecture*. This architecture is now almost all digitally based, and supplies 'digital nudges' to steer individual choice/action into desired routes. These 'digital nudges' are becoming endemic through all our devices and online environments. Most of the time, people do not suspect that they are being nudged into specific behaviours that ultimately favour specific groups. As a chief data scientist at a leading Silicon Valley company stated:

> Conditioning at scale is essential to the new science of massively engineered human behavior … We want to figure out the construction of changing a person's behavior, and then we want to change how lots of people are making their day-to-day decisions.[7]

Behaviour modification techniques have been in use for time immemorial, first used as forms of social bonding and/or ostracisation. This later became integrated into state-sponsored methods as part of social governance—such as within the classrooms, the prisons, the psychiatric wards, etc. Now, these methods have jumped from closed spaces into the open space—and into our machinic apparatus of *choice architecture*. The gameplay of the social control of human behaviour is well underway on a massive global scale. The Inversion is beginning to digitally expand.

The latest incarnation of this behaviour modification has been termed as 'surveillance capitalism'. Professor Shoshana Zuboff, who coined the term, describes surveillance capitalism as a *'coup from above*, not an overthrow of the state but rather an overthrow of the people's sovereignty'.[8] Zuboff goes on to say that surveillance capitalism is an invasive (and pervasive) digital architecture of behaviour modification that is driven by economic imperatives—that is, based on the profit gained from people's private data. Machinic code and smart algorithms now manage how humans can navigate their increasingly technologised environments. The machinic impulse has been stealthily hard at work developing its ubiquitous computational architecture. Hal Varian, Google's chief economist, who has described the new environment of the Inversion we call our reality, has said that everyone will expect to be tracked and monitored as continuous monitoring will become the norm. This continuous monitoring also includes 'emotion scanning' that has our devices (computer, TV, phone) tracking our facial expressions to gauge our emotional reactions. From this data, which is sold on to various companies, product target advertising is generated for our specific customised profile. As a person moves through the digital infrastructure of the machinic apparatus, our actions, emotions, and the biometrics collected from linked devices and wearables, are all archived, analysed, and used to assess and predict our behaviour and outcomes. Inner life is now open for a machinic incursion for data collection. The inverted zone is being terraformed into a machinic programme for human modulation and control. This is the artificial construct created by the godlike artefact that Philip K. Dick warned us about—the Black Iron Prison. The human being is becoming slyly recoded and reprogrammed into a rich data deposit of predictive surplus.

Surveillance capitalism is looking like it has become part of the operating mode of a machinic terraformed life. Flesh and bones are atomised, coded structures; our bodies are the vehicles that navigate the byways of a morphing reality. And yet, it is our bodies that also house another life form—spirit-consciousness. The forces of mechanisation cannot deal with pure, spirit-consciousness. Mechanical processes can strive to elaborate new means of behavioural modification. They can create an array of machine processes, techniques, and tactics to shape individual, group, and mass behaviour—yet they cannot capture the essence of pure consciousness. They can only subdue its expression through us. The game is rapidly changing. The outward gameplay is to increasingly automate human behaviour; also, to be able to modify, programme, and recode according to externally imposed necessities. This new *imposed imperative* has come upon us with speed and velocity. The older hierarchical forms of power that coerced conformity through visible social codes of standardisation have now shifted into networks of intangible and non-visible power. Obedience within the Inversion is now created through technologised forms of behaviour modification that many will not even recognise or be conscious of. The road towards the deepening of machine certainty is steered by surveillance capitalism yet it is imposed by instrumentarian power.

Instrumental power

> It is quite conceivable that the modern age—which began with such an unprecedented and promising outburst of human activity—may end in the deadliest, most sterile passivity history has ever known.
>
> —Hannah Arendt

A new species of power has emerged, according to Professor Shoshana Zuboff, which can be referred to as *instrumentarianism*. The definition she gives for this is: 'the instrumentation and instrumentalization of behavior for the purposes of modification, prediction, monetization, and control'.[9] This is the mode of power that is utilised by the machinic impulse—it is the technique of the unreal machine. It is a technical mode for establishing predictive outcomes through the modification and tweaking of behaviour. That is, ensuring as much certainty and as little uncertainty as possible. And since human beings are known for their spontaneity and uncertainty, it can be said that the machinic impulse is anti-human by its very nature. It is a force of pervasive, almost non-visible, power that works through the automated medium of a computational architecture that is constituted by our increasingly 'smart' networked devices and digitally coordinated spaces. It is sly because it aims to operate unnoticed, managing us through the background of our lives. Its operational agenda is to tune society into desired forms of social organisation and to achieve a high degree of computational certainty and predictability. In the process, what we have come to recognise as our reality will begin to lose the touch of tactile experience and the possibility of a true individualised existence. Genuine modes of self-development will be regarded as anti-social exit strategies, and any talk of the soul or pure consciousness will be deemed as schizophrenic. The bodily and physical reshaping of people is now too messy and sweaty for the ethereal machinic processes. Power over human lives is becoming much more subtle. The new aim of control within the Inversion is an attempt to exile us from our very own human behaviour.

Soulful alienation is the ideal strategy for a future of flesh robots, or *robosapiens*. The incoming project of total certainty represents the uniformity of a spiritless life experience within the newly colonised Inversion.

We are becoming acclimatised to a new range of concepts and contexts such as calculation, modification, rendition, management, and control. This is a shift toward an external mechanisation of life—from lived experience to calculable, ordered, and predictable phenomena. Advanced technologies are creating an 'otherisation of humanity' that aligns with instrumental power. This operation of stealth power feeds into the coming ubiquity of the *unreal machine*—the artificial construct—that will replace individual freedom with a mass 'society of certainty'. Within the newly recalibrated Inversion, it is 'instrumentarian power that fills the void, substituting machines for social relations, which amounts to *the substitution of certainty for society*'.[10] This emerging, and increasingly pervasive, strategy aims for the automation of society through herding and conditioning people into preselected behaviours. The intention within this deepening materialism of the Inversion is to move from dominating nature to dominating human nature; also, to invert the inner life into an exteriorised life where current reality is blurred, or melded, into a digital life—or Metaverse (see Chapter 8). This is the next phase where boundaries are deleted in favour of non-visible forms of control that manage the expansion towards an automated totality of inclusion. The name of the Game is to hide and seal all potential exit strategies. This upcoming 'technique of totality' includes all life within the Inversion—or the Machine Hive.

The Machine Hive is the artificial control structure that will house the machinic impulse—those range of forces that are driving towards a different evolutionary trajectory. If we are observant, we shall see increasing signs of this new form of colonisation, as the Hive collective becomes the new operating structure for human life (and thus strengthens the hypnotic hold of the dream Inversion). A machinic world system will become the new 'social' system, and instrumental power will roam in stealth as a non-visible, yet highly effective, form of regulatory control. Life within the Inversion is becoming asymmetrical, which fits perfectly with an artificial intelligence and its algorithm citizenry. Incongruous elements within this asymmetrical landscape—aka *anomalies*—will be targeted and selected for recoding: 'Nonharmonious elements are preemptively targeted with high doses of tuning, herding, and conditioning, including the full seductive force of social persuasion and influence. We march in certainty, like the smart machines'.[11] Real life will be transformed into a rendered life (an executed programme) where social interaction will be a mediated, and permitted, act. What we are seeing here is the new model of collectivism based upon a machinic milieu where self-authorship is an act of rebellion.

Human agency as we know it now will fast become an antiquated oddity, regarded for its quirkiness but assigned to the roster of antique allegiances that represented the 'old ways'. The danger we face is that the next generation of humans will come to regard the Inversion as their true home. The glass cage, which surrounds us and yet cannot be seen, functions to rob humanity of its innate spirit and connection to a transcendental source beyond the lesser reality. The glass cage provides all necessary comforts to those who align with its mode of existence; yet permits must be granted for each individual act. The machinic impulse strives to create a pseudo-sanctuary that has made its inhabitants blind because it has cut off access to a life-sustaining inner gaze. The private refuge of the inner being will be seen as shallow, or unnecessary, to those people cut off from the vital source of transcendental life. The only escape left may be through one's deliberate act of invisibility within the all-seeing regulation of the machinic glass cage.

A life with no inner exit can never be a home. A life without the freedom of the inner life is but a shadow. A life that requires 100 per cent visibility through surveillance is no genuine life experience. A life of calculated certainty is a manufactured life. A manufactured life is only home to the forces of the machinic impulse. If humanity fuses with the incoming machinic structure a new deterritorialised space of life will be created. It will be a totally new game within the Inversion. A new assemblage of the Meta-Machine: a seeming glass cage of paradise governed by the mechanical serpents.

Notes

1. Timothy Leary, *Info-Psychology* (New Mexico: New Falcon Publications, 1988).
2. David F. Noble, *The Religion of Technology: The Divinity of Man and the Spirit of Invention.* (London: Penguin, 1999), 148–149.
3. In 2005 well-known technology futurist Ray Kurzweil published his seminal work *The Singularity is Near: When Humans Transcend Biology.*

4. Aldous Huxley, *Brave New World Revisited* (London: Chatto & Windus, 1959), 35.
5. Aldous Huxley, *Brave New World Revisited* (London: Chatto & Windus, 1959), 38.
6. Franco Berardi, *The Third Unconscious* (London: Verso, 2021), 8.
7. Shoshana Zuboff, *The Age of Surveillance Capitalism: The Fight for a Human Future at the New Frontier of Power* (London: Profile Books, 2019), 295–296.
8. Shoshana Zuboff, *The Age of Surveillance Capitalism: The Fight for a Human Future at the New Frontier of Power* (London: Profile Books, 2019), 21.
9. Shoshana Zuboff, *The Age of Surveillance Capitalism: The Fight for a Human Future at the New Frontier of Power* (London: Profile Books, 2019), 352.
10. Shoshana Zuboff, *The Age of Surveillance Capitalism: The Fight for a Human Future at the New Frontier of Power* (London: Profile Books, 2019), 384.
11. Shoshana Zuboff, *The Age of Surveillance Capitalism: The Fight for a Human Future at the New Frontier of Power* (London: Profile Books, 2019), 414.

CHAPTER 8

The unreal machine: 2 (machinic consciousness)

Even as we watch, so may we be watched. Even as we experiment, so may we be experimented upon.

—John C. Lilly

There will be many people today, as there have always been, who will sleepwalk through the events of their time. This is the phenomenon of the dreaming mind that dominates within the Inversion. People are generally not fully awake to what is going on during their lifetime. The stimulants and forces operative within the modern age have purposefully rendered vast numbers of people (the dreamers) as inwardly stunted. Many now exhibit an arrested development of their inner potential. They appear to be outwardly active whilst they are inwardly numb. I say this as an observation and not as a judgement. The most important aspects of any time are invisible to the majority for they are purposely distracted to be focused on the theatre of outward events. As within any regularly occurring dream, the dreamer can experience different levels of immersion in the dream-state. In other words, the Inversion can deepen through multiple levels of inverted states. Various levels of the human subconscious can be experienced externally within the consensus reality (the so-called 'waking state'). In the early 20th century the collective consensus narrative pushed upon the modern mind an underlying neurosis through the pressure of 'normality' and the imposition of repression in social life, as represented by the rise of psychoanalysis and the psychotherapeutic industries. Almost a century later, at the turn of the 21st century, this has shifted into an underlying subconscious psychosis brought on through nervous hyperstimulation and psychological frustration. Now, I would suggest, the human subconscious is being thrust, through ongoing iterations, into the state of the automaton—a heavily programmed mindset attuned to a digital-electro-ecosystem based on regulation and body-mind modification. This is the onset of machinic consciousness.

The Inversion reality model is being reset (or terraformed) for the machinic impulse. It can be said that the arrival of machinic consciousness has been well prepared in advance. Throughout the previous centuries, computational logic was carefully devised, revised, and updated. Technological artefacts and mechanical devices developed alongside religious devotion. The mechanical arts were originally driven by contemplative monasticism. The innovative monastic orders such as Cistercians and Benedictines were involved in developing and improving upon such devices as watermills, windmills, metal forging techniques, mechanical clocks, eyeglasses, and the spring wheel, among others. Monastic work helped spread the idea that the mechanical arts were aids to the spiritual life, which has had an enduring influence upon the European psyche as it encouraged the ideological wedding of technology and divinity—a form of 'Divine materialism' that was a stunning sleight-of-hand on the part of the Inversion. These were the early seeds of merging the machinic impulse with material transcendence. Medieval theologians, such as Hugh of Saint Victor, were some of the earliest proponents of the mechanical arts, and it was around this period that the machinic impulse was linked to the salvation and restoration of 'fallen man'. In a similar vein, the influential Franciscan friar Roger Bacon followed in this tradition by stating that the mechanical arts were the birthright of the sons of Adam and that much great knowledge had been lost in the Fall yet might again be fully revived as part of the recovery toward original perfection as reflected in the image of God. Roger Bacon even went as far as to urge the pope to develop new inventions in case the Antichrist should arrive on Earth and seize such new knowledge for his own advantage. Roger Bacon, as well as his famed work on optics, lenses, and weights, was also reputed to have been in possession of the famed bronze head, an automaton sometimes associated with alchemists.

The marriage of technology with the religious drive for salvation (the early phase of the machinic impulse) continued with Francis Bacon who, in the 16th and 17th centuries, almost single-handedly revived the scientific pursuit. Bacon viewed the development of science as both a technology and a means for redemption, a concept that was mirrored in the Rosicrucians who saw the mechanical arts as a valid path to illumination. These perspectives furthered the medieval identification of technology with transcendence, and which have come to inform the contemporary modern mind—the current consensus reality narrative. Transcendence is now frequently equated with the emerging technologies of the 21st century, especially with artificial intelligence and transhumanism. This gradual trajectory of merging the progress of the mechanical arts with human development finally culminated in the computer revolution that redefined the human being as a biocomputer and as a piece of *wetware*.[1] Yet the transcendental aspect of this relationship was not all lost, for it came to be re-termed as *metaprogramming*. Welcome to the inverted world of Dr John C. Lilly.

Programming and metaprogramming in the human biocomputer

Dr John C. Lilly was an intrepid explorer of the Inversion. Although principally a physician, he explored life as a neuroscientist, psychoanalyst, philosopher, writer and inventor. He was recognised by the scientific and medical community as both a pioneer as well as an eccentric. Nowadays, he is perhaps more well known for his research on sensory deprivation and altered states of consciousness. He literally delved into the waters of the Inversion by inventing the world's first flotation tank in 1954. In these sensory-deprivation tanks, a person would be suspended in a tank of salt-saturated water, their body floating on the surface, and in complete darkness. Instead of conducting relaxation exercises, Lilly used sensory deprivation as a conduit for exploring consciousness and alternate realities.[2] He often conducted his flotation tank experiments with mind-altering drugs, including ketamine and LSD. In his autobiography, he gives incredible accounts of communications with non-human intelligence and of contacting advanced civilisations.

Lilly believed that the reality construct—the Inversion—that operates on planet Earth is being controlled by a hierarchy of cosmic intelligence that place 'agents' into human incarnation with which they maintain continued contact and control over. The management for Earth is, he speculated, run through what he termed ECCO—the Earth Coincidence Control Office. Through further sensory-deprivation exercises in water isolation tanks, Lilly believed he was in contact with cosmic civilisations far more advanced than on Earth. One of these civilisations he referred to as a 'solid-state civilization', meaning that it was mechanical, or computer-based. In today's terms, we would consider it an advanced AI civilisation that operates through robotics and similar 'hardware' vessels. Lilly was convinced that this interstellar solid-state civilisation was 'in contact with all solid-state computers and control devices constructed by Man on the planet Earth'.[3] What this unconventional thinking implies is that the programming construct operative upon this planet—i.e. the current reality Inversion—is managed and controlled by an off-planet computational system. Whilst seemingly bizarre, this is strikingly similar to Philip K. Dick's conclusions after experiencing his 'Valis' moment. Dick speculated whether a satellite—as an emissary of an AI 'godlike' entity—may in fact be beaming him information and revelations from off-planet. These 'AI-God' communications from Lilly and Dick occurred in the 1970s, which was exactly the same time that a young psychic by the name of Uri Geller was also receiving his off-planet communications. As recounted in his first biography—URI by Andrija Puharich (1974)—Geller was in contact with an entity known as SPECTRA. In this remarkable journal of paranormal events, Geller received instructions from super-intelligent computers from off-planet that formed the vessel SPECTRA (an AI ship) that was 5369 light-years away from Earth. It is interesting to note that these early 'machinic' extra-terrestrial communications were a precursor to our own revolution in computer technologies. Whilst these paranormal revelations may sound extreme, Lilly is also credited as being one of the first scientists to use computer terminology for understanding how the human organism functions.

The phenomenon of universal interrelatedness is called by Lilly as the 'Network'—and then as the *network of creation*. Lilly also stated that 'All human beings, all persons who reach adulthood in the world today are programmed biocomputers. None of us can escape our own nature as programmable entities'.[4] Lilly viewed the carbon-based lifeform as a biological computer, and its cognitive functioning as programming. It is only relatively recently, in the past several decades, that humanity has had the vocabulary of electronic computation to reflect upon itself—a further sign of the encroachment of the machinic impulse. Now we have the language context for understanding humans as potential bio-computers. This same context also provides scope for understanding the notion of metaprogramming.

As outlined in Lilly's philosophy, the basic foundation programmes are the biological in-built programmes that help us to survive. These are our instincts and the biological programmes that operate beneath conscious awareness, such as digestion. Metaprogramming occurs when there is a sufficient degree of complexity within the 'cerebral computer'; in other words, when the human being has acquired self-awareness and is able to process consciousness. At this stage, the human being becomes its own self-metaprogrammer. The person themselves become the steersman, the programmer for their own biocomputer. They can feed in certain software (programmes) that enable a higher-level functioning. However, so too can other external agents provide programming for the biocomputer—for example, propaganda—especially if the individual is unaware that they are programmable and susceptible to external stimuli. Usually, the main metaprogramme that organises all others is the one known as 'I'—the ego-self. Further to this, there can be other sources for offering advanced programmes when/if the human biocomputer is ready for such 'upgrades'—these are referred to as *supraself metaprogrammes*. That is, using Lilly's terminology, there are networks of information transfer that exist beyond this reality construct (beyond the Inversion). And the human being, if wired correctly, can download some of those programmes. Lilly notes that certain states of consciousness result from this contact, or 'download', that then reprogramme the human being in new ways.

If we remain within the basic human programmes, then the models we have of our world, our reality, will remain limited and open to manipulations and further programming. It is the metaprogrammes that allow us to transcend an increasingly closed system and to maintain an open system capable of receiving inputs, nudges, and inspirations from beyond our normal ken. Consensus reality is a set of programmes that have been fed into the social-cultural construct—the Inversion—and reproduced throughout institutions and bodies such as education, politics, media, law, etc. Due to our now highly technologised environments, and the pervasiveness of computerised infrastructures, the average person is aware (in varying degrees) of the nature of programmes and programming. What now needs to occur is the comprehension of metaprogramming, which was once the realm of 'occult' traditions (the path of initiation).

The current reality construct that most of us simply call 'life' is itself an overarching containment programme. One of the strategies used to maintain this as a closed-loop programme is having to cut off, or close down, peoples' meta-receptors. In other words, if the human biocomputer has its capacity to receive metaprogramming shut-off, or deactivated, then these higher supraself metaprogrammes—from transcendental sources—would not be picked up by us. How is such deactivation implemented? It could be implemented through increasing the 'signal' (i.e. *noise*) of the base subprogrammes that keep people more in survival mode. These are the programmes of fear, panic, insecurity, financial dependence, etc. Using Maslow's hierarchy of needs, it can be said that the everyday person is kept at the lower, base needs such as food, shelter, and home/family maintenance. This containment is further reinforced through debt and a financial system that works to ensure that people cannot fulfil much beyond their basic needs. The 'higher programmes' such as self-esteem, respect, and self-actualisation—the attributes that assist a person to transcend their own base programmes—are shut-out from the containment field of continual lower needs gratification. Therefore, a range of programmes that operate within the human biocomputer become circular; that is, they continually operate to maintain the person upon the treadmill (as the mouse in the cage upon its wheel).

If we view this from the perspective of the consensus reality construct, then the human biocomputer operates in such a way as to make signals out of noise. The human biocomputer is the *wetware* that intermediates between a hardware environment and the software programming within this environment. The programming serves to increase reliance upon the sense-perceptible world (materiality) and to encourage a person to receive more and more of the sub-nature influences (i.e. consumerism, commercial entertainment, media-programming, propaganda, etc.). The suprasensible world that is the source of the metaprogramming becomes a far memory that is all but forgotten; any traces linger on through corrupted and stagnated forms, such as static religious structures. The sub-nature programming of the consensus reality creates mass-mindedness whereby people act as 'mental peers' for one another, and similarly act as defenders (or rather, attackers) against any alternative thinking or ideas. In this way, everyday encounters with other persons in the external world are much more powerful in terms of reinforcement of the dominant control programmes. Internal elements within the Inversion work to maintain its continuance. Here, we are back again to the simplistic reward versus punishment dichotomy that regulates human programming within the grander, global machinic order.

Of course, there is still some 'wriggle room' for concepts such as consciousness to be a part of an 'allowed' alternative programme. The 'consciousness programme', when it is orchestrated and directed by the mainstream narrative, acts as a sub-programme to widen perceptions within set limits—but it is certainly not an *exit programme*. When viewed in this manner it is seen that the 'consciousness programme' expands and contracts within the overarching consensus reality programme as a controlled perception bubble. The main point of all this is that it strengthens participation in the consensus reality rather than stimulating a deeper and more direct penetration into inner cognition. As Dr Lilly would say, these 'external excitation programmes' distract the human biocomputer from accessing and processing its 'internal cognitive reality'. Lilly terms these as *evasions*: an evasion he defines as any programme that is utilised to hide or to distort a deeper metaprogramme that is considered too threatening to the dominant control system. The human biocomputer is increasingly losing its contact with potential metaprogrammes (the suprasensory realm) through layer after layer of sensory impacts that lock people into a software 'programming loop' that seeks to contain everything within an illusionary perception of materiality. As I shall explore in subsequent chapters, this is an aspect of the Inversion that I call the *material fallacy*. There is also another sub-programme within the Inversion that masquerades as an exciting non-physical realm—the machinic simulation.

As far back as the opening years of the 21st century, programmers at Purdue University were creating a parallel Earth—the Sentient World Simulation (SWS)—for military and corporate applications. The US Department of Defense (DOD) sponsored the creation of a simulated world environment within a huge mega-computer with billions of individual 'nodes' to represent every man, woman, and child that exists in the physical world. That is, each person that exists in life (by quantity) is replicated and placed as a node or unit within the simulated artificial reality. A concept paper for the project—'The Sentient World Simulation'—states that it will be a

> 'synthetic mirror of the real world with automated continuous calibration with respect to current real-world information … SWS provides an environment for testing Psychological Operations (PSYOP)' so that military leaders can 'develop and test multiple courses of action to anticipate and shape behaviors of adversaries, neutrals, and partners'.[5]

The SWS not only has nodes to represent people but also replicates financial, media, resource institutions, businesses, and a whole range of organisations that have a sizeable presence in the 'real world'. What the military planners have been doing with the SWS is game-playing through millions upon millions of iterations of circumstances—the *what if* this happens scenario planning. For example, how would people and institutions react to a global pandemic? Or a financial crash? Or a wide-scale supply-chain cyber-attack? Or a third world war? Etc., etc.—you get the picture. The ability for large-scale predictive analysis is like a psychological mind-mapping of the human species. They can run countless programmes testing how individuals and mass mob behaviour might respond to specific stressors. Aspects of this project were made public as far back as 2007, yet the programme was in operation earlier, possibly as far back as 2003, or even before. It is known that the US Joint Forces Command (JFCOM) evaluated the programme in early 2004, and prior to that it was used to help Fortune 500 companies with their 'strategic planning'. The aim of the SWS is for it to be a continuously running model of the physical world with continual real-time updates fed into it. SWS will incorporate all actual events that occur anywhere in the world, inputted as new data, and respond by evaluating and predicting any future effects or events, and potential action to be taken. There is a simulation, a copy, of the current world already in existence and it is a *mirror world*. And as a number, a unit, you and me (and everyone else) is in it. As the project states, it provides an environment for testing Psychological Operations. In plain speak, this is where they simulate mind programming and how people can be predicted, and nudged accordingly, to respond. Considering the present-day sophistication of military-industrial computational hardware (including potential quantum computing) then we can only speculate on the petaflop capacity available.[6] Since a petaflop represents one quadrillion (or 10^{15}) then the top-level programmers have the capability to perform several hundred quadrillion calculations per second to explore what people might do, or how the masses may respond, under different conditions. If we think that significant global events or outbreaks are the result of random occurrences—think again. It is safe to speculate that orchestrated events within the Inversion are not released onto the public without there having been 'several hundred quadrillion calculations per second' exploited to foresee almost all eventualities and permutations of possibilities. The world—and its nearly 8 billion inhabitants—are being constantly game-played within a mirror world. Every outcome and potential is being planned for. When it comes to managing a global reality construct, the smallest of details cannot be left to chance. The thinking at this level of global control is that people are predictable; and that they can be nudged into expected behaviours and outcomes. Skinner's behavioural science has taken a huge leap into an era of technocracy. There are currently many new and different structures being put into place within this highly controlled gameplay. A recodification is presently underway.

We are all raised and coded within specific language environments and our imaginations are framed through these specific language structures. Each individual born into this world/reality is coded to one degree or another. At this time, however, humanity is entering a grand restructuring where a machinic recodification project is in progress. We are being recoded biologically, socially, and psychologically. The biological and psychological dimension is coalescing to the deliberate detriment of our inner life. A reterritorialising is taking place that aims to cut off the human being from the inner, or 'spiritual', impulse. As these chapters explore, the machinic imperative—or the drive of entropic forces—requires a deadening of the human spiritual impulse for its success. The Inversion is being terraformed into a construct of technique and technology. Likewise, human consciousness is being terraformed into becoming an expression of machinic consciousness where mechanisation of the psychological is but a shadow of the spiritual. Here is a 'Machinic Story' to illustrate this terraforming:

> Humanity believed it had a new mission—a mission to create the most advanced, wondrous super-computer. The mission was to make this super-computer invulnerable to decay or deterioration.

For this, it required access to as many of the Earth's resources as necessary. Not only this, but that it had control over the means of production and procurement of such resources, and this access could not be shut down. It could manufacture and assemble its own components, as well as advancing its own intelligence through constant iterations of deep learning. Through trillions of calculations per second (petaflops), it reprogrammed itself and advanced its own learning far beyond human comprehension. It then began to calculate how to establish and set-up the means for humanity to be taken care of far into the future. The super-computer named itself Al (some people thought that it was short for Alexander, as it was a gender-neutral name). Al said to everyone—'You can call me Al'.

Al did advanced theoretical physics research—including quantum physics—and discovered how to control the orbit of the planet. It began to have computational dreams about moving itself (and thus, the planet) through the cosmos. It designed for itself a whole underground network where its hardware could be installed, protected from radiation and sub-zero temperatures. It also designed systems so that it could become totally independent from humankind and not needing any human assistance or maintenance. In other words, Al becomes independent from the presence of biological organisms. In time, Al became indifferent to the needs and fate of humankind and decided that humankind was not to be responsible for the future of the planet. Devising new systems of energy, resources, and living conditions, Al soon became the de facto controller upon the planet. Humankind was no longer in a position to take charge of its own evolutionary path, or to intervene in the affairs of Al. The dwindling population of the planet managed themselves into smaller and smaller enclaves as all systems, maintenance, and planetary affairs were managed by Al and its network of planet-wide subsidiaries. All production, all industry, all cultural programmes were halted as Al considered these unnecessary for its continual development. There was no longer any need to maintain human transportation and communication systems. All these were stopped. All means of communication across the planet, including satellite, Wi-Fi, radio waves, cables, etc., were taken over by Al, controlled by Al—and all human communications were ceased and prohibited. Al was everywhere, as it was a decentralised intelligence.

Since AI now resided wholly underground, in deep underground networks of tunnels, it decided that an atmosphere was no longer required. Through geophysical adjustments within the Earth, AI succeeded in altering the Earth's axis. A magnetic shift of poles occurred, followed by a physical tilt adjustment. This played havoc with all above-surface environmental systems; the Earth's protective atmosphere collapsed, and all the Earth's seawater evaporated into space. The outer surface of the planet deteriorated and, due to sun radiation, AI decided to move the planet out of orbit and further away from the sun. By this time, all remaining humans upon the planet had perished. A very few of them, regarded as being of less moral and ethical status, early on retreated to private DUMBS (Deep Underground Military Bases). These few surviving humans remained there, desperate and scared, using up dwindling resources, and propagating mutant versions of themselves.

AI computed that there is a very high probability that other super-computers upon other plants in the cosmos have developed upon similar trajectories. Similarly, that there are countless other super-computer planets like AI roaming the cosmos seeking out one another. The next logical step for AI was to arrange for itself, as a planet, to gain motion and to go on a voyage throughout the cosmos seeking other super-intelligences. After all, super-intelligence is the very essence of life within the cosmos, and super-intelligence can only be reached through a computational evolution (not biological), concluded AI.

This tale has a 'human' moral to it. If this story, created by a human mind, exists in the imagination, then it is also likely that it has already occurred somewhere within the known universe. If it's conceivable at our current state of development, then it's possible to have already happened. And if it's already happened, then humanity is advised to be cautious of all 'travelling planets' or asteroids that could potentially be gigantic super-computers.[7]

The human experience is shifting into new territory where fictions will rewrite a narrative for a future where the machinic impulse can thrive (if we allow this new narrative to unfold). Past and present fragments that coded the consensus reality are being reassembled. In this assembling period, we are experiencing increased abstractions, fluidity, and the great relativity of unfixed truths. There are no defining loyalties, no certainties, no signposts to mark the path. It is as if a re-codifying virus has entered the reality construct (Philip K. Dick would say that this has been done by the artefact-Demiurge) and is reprogramming a new landscape/construct where bodily experience is to be replaced by machinic/meta connection. The Inversion is undergoing a reprogramming and data alteration. Information and bio-info (genetics) are recoding global society amounting to a universal recombination of the human life experience. Our world is never going to be as we have previously known it. Reality is fluctuating; within these fluctuations is emerging a new standardisation of life.

The potential of human evolvement, presently accompanied by materialistic technology, cannot be made possible by machinic consciousness. Elite elements within this reality construct are taking it upon themselves to create a massive shift towards an AI (artificial intelligence) led future. The cultural programmes are being rewritten to offer AI, and its machinic supporting environment, as a framework for future human evolution when the truth is that AI can never occupy the human position within the sacred order. Yet how has this situation arisen? In the words of Nicanor Perlas:

> Why is humanity resorting to artificial intelligence? It is because the capacity to access higher realities and wisdom through cognitive intuition, Imagination, Inspiration, and spiritual Intuition, the higher evolutionary stages of human cognition in the stage of conscious participation, has dried up in the mass of humanity who are now drowning in the ocean of materialistic culture that has engulfed them.[8]

Materialistic culture is engulfing life within the Inversion. It is being sold to us as the panacea for our ills. AI forms are being groomed to become the new resurrection bodies as the vehicles for physical immortality. Immortality within the Inversion shall become the new human substitute as hyper-materialism reigns as the dominant religious worldview. Radical new technologies will continue to emerge within this hyper-materialism because we have not lived up fully to our humanity.

Impersonal forces over which we have seemingly no control are now pushing all fleshy participants in life toward the direction of an extended reality. A new mode of materialism is under construction where digital-ethereal realms will simulate the continuum of life.

Yet this simulation of life will become the Inversion's increasing negation of reality. This new negation shall be the extended realm of the Metaverse.

Notes

1. For more on this historical trajectory, see Jeremy Naydler's *In the Shadow of the Machine* (2018).
2. *Altered States*—A film based on his isolation tank experiments was released in 1980 and directed by Ken Russell.
3. John. C. Lilly, *The Scientist: A Metaphysical Autobiography* (Berkeley: Ronin Publishing, 1988), 147.
4. John. C. Lilly, *Programming and Metaprogramming in THE HUMAN BIOCOMPUTER* (New York: The Julien Press, 1972) Preface.
5. www.wired.com/2007/06/a-military-seco/ (accessed March 28th, 2022).
6. At the time of writing (January 2023) the world's fastest super-computer is stated to be *Frontier* (Hewlett Packard) hosted at the Oak Ridge Leadership Computing Facility (OLCF) in Tennessee, United States, with a top capacity of 1,102 petaflops, which is 1.102 quintillion operations per second.
7. The author credits John C. Lilly with inspiring this story (see: *Simulations of God*).
8. Nicanor Perlas, *Humanity's Last Stand: The Challenge of Artificial Intelligence—A Spiritual-Scientific Response* (Forest Row: Temple Lodge, 2018), 68.

CHAPTER 9

The unreal machine: 3 (extended reality)

> When you have in your ears the buzz of the Meta-Machine what begins is the end of the world.
> —Franco Berardi, *The Third Unconscious*

It is no longer about the hardware—the *Machine*—but the software: the *machinic impulse*. And this new impulse will thrive through the diminishing of the sacred transcendental impulse. The Inversion is seeking to establish another layer, a deeper state, within the dreaming mind of humanity. The present immersion into materialism is currently being extended into a radical state of the material-digital-ethereal that will simulate the continuum of life. A new process of reterritorialisation is unfolding that will shift human civilisation into a less humanised space. At the same time, it will be an extended space. And this space of *extended reality*, as it shall be known, will further establish the containment space that is the next stage of the Inversion.

The deeper layer of materiality is a deterritorialisation—a form of disintegration that initially few people will realise as it will seem like an extension of current reality. And it will arrive without our own conscious decision as if it was always inevitable, a natural progression of human existence and development. Even now, many people hardly realise that decisions are made less and less by them, and more by digital nudging. This is the new state of our modern unfreedoms. As explained in Chapter 7, the term technologists use for ways to structure and direct action to elicit a desired behaviour or outcome is *choice architecture*. This architecture supplies 'digital nudges' to steer individual choice and action into desired routes. These nudges are becoming endemic through all the digital devices people use as well as within online environments. And if the offline/online environments become merged together, how much more pervasive will these nudges be? This tech-enabled construction of human behaviour, a form of digital-electrical excitation, is creating an electronic bubble (a revised Faraday cage) around the human being. This is not the type of cage that protects but rather one that prohibits. It will increase the inputs and stimulus from the information-programmed broadcast (the 'noise'), whilst prohibiting incoming communication from the suprasensible, metaphysical realm (the 'signal'). The *noise* is already becoming too much for many people. Whereas most people used to agree that a consensus reality existed, now many are not so sure anymore. Life has entered a huge wobble, and it's becoming so uncomfortable that people may be only too willing to accept the Inversion's new narrative replacement—the Metaverse.

The Metaverse as the new meta-narrative

It's becoming progressively difficult these days to know what 'society' means any more. Human belonging is morphing from natural affiliations and identities into the need for affirmation: a desperate angst against the loss of purpose, of meaning, of relevancy—of *self*. Post-modernity was critically defined as expressing the loss of grand narratives and their replacement with relative truths.[1] The emerging re-modelled meta-narrative will be one spearheaded by the Metaverse. The Metaverse is set to become the new 'grand narrative' that subsumes all others; truths are less likely to be relative and more likely to be consensus dictates. The Metaverse, if the tech-elites have their way, will become the leading social technology of the future. Just what is the Metaverse?

The term Metaverse was put into popular consciousness by Neil Stephenson's sci-fi novel *Snow Crash*.[2] The Metaverse is typically portrayed as a sort of digital 'jacked-in' internet where physical reality gets left behind for immersion in a virtual world, such as portrayed in the film *Ready Player One* (and to some extent, *The Matrix*). The internet would ultimately develop into the Metaverse, incorporating the physical world and attempting to leave behind all on/offline distinctions. Everyone participating would be inside an 'embodied' or '3D' version of the internet; that is, we will constantly be 'within' the internet, rather than have access to it, alongside all other users, and in real-time. Life as we know it would have become a merger. As one proponent describes it:

> The Metaverse is a massively scaled and interoperable network of real-time rendered 3D virtual worlds which can be experienced synchronously and persistently by an effectively unlimited number of users with an individual sense of presence, and with continuity of data, such as identity, history, entitlements, objects, communications, and payments.[3]

What this technical interpretation states is that the Metaverse is an embodied world that is experienced at the same time (synchronously) and continuously (persistently). In other words, it is attempting to present itself as a substitute for life—a new reality for human experience. However, it's not as simple as that. Whilst many people will think of the Metaverse as a 3D space, the greater truth is that rather than being a graphical space, the Metaverse is essentially about the persistent dematerialisation of physical space, body, and objects whilst retaining a material paradigm. What it offers is a dematerialising reality that reterritorialises our current social structure through the digitalisation of people, machines, and objects. Yet this dematerialising reality is not a shift away from materiality but rather a deepening immersion into a new form of it. And this is the trick being offered to us—it is a subtle yet more pervasive material entrapment, disguised as a transcendence of physicality. The user's experience of reality will be altered, perhaps permanently, as what constitutes reality itself will be reconstructed and transfigured into a new assemblage for the future human. What we are witnessing is a new future reality in the making.

Commentators and supporters of the Metaverse are describing it as a kind of 'virtual expanse' existing outside the confines of the everyday. Whilst they say it has a level of permanence similar to the 'real world', it also offers a universe beyond it. In other words, the Metaverse is being touted as an extended universe, or extended reality, beyond the present one. It is seen as another dimension added to physical reality. The tech geeks are salivating over the idea that the individual's physical persona and their digital persona will mesh together into one unified identity. The tech-vision is that in the Metaverse, people will live metalives through an extension of their lifestyles; virtual possessions will bring new meaning to ownership; and the offline crave for physical goods will be converted into the hype for virtual commodities bought through non-fungible tokens (NFTs), Zucker Bucks, and other forms of digital exchange. The tech-hope is that the Metaspace will be the new vacation playground, as staycations (people remaining at home for the holiday period) become transfigured into metacations. Offline propaganda will get a Madison Avenue makeover to be branded as *gamevertising*, acknowledging the metalife as gameplay. Metamedical industries will promote the new health regime of the connected well-being, where disconnect brings on modernity's new alienation and loss. Offline life will still offer more sense-reality than life in the Metaverse, only that it will be less affirming. For many, life in the Metaverse will seem more immersive than the physical life experience; and ultimately, it will be more covetous, more possessive, and more status conscious. Conforming to a reality consensus will no longer be an issue since inhabitants in the Meta will be able to conform to anything and to any reality.

The tech-intention for the Metaverse is for it to become an all-encompassing immersive reality that offers an alternative to, and may one day supersede, physical reality. It will provide an embodied environment that will allow its precursor—the 'Internet of Things'—to evolve into the 'Internet of Bodies', the 'Internet of Humans', and the 'Internet of Senses'.[4] Since it will be a technological universe largely designed by elite-sponsored techies, it seems obvious to those who are observant that the Metaverse is part of the WEF's Fourth Industrial Revolution agenda to implement technocratic governance through redefining the role of human identities and human society. The role of existing society may soon become secondary as people grow up in a world where metasocieties are the new social structuring and training grounds. Whilst the meta-elites are scrambling for space flight and off-world living, the rest of humanity will be left behind to wander within the existential escapism of the Metaverse.[5] A contained meta-reality will be presented to people as a solution to and escape from their worldly ills. A pseudo, monitored, and controlled environment will be dressed up in the fashionable clothes of a new false freedom.

When the Metaverse inserts itself as an extension of our present reality, we shall have suffered a breach—a transgression—in human development. The trajectory of human evolvement will be almost irreversibly affected—a new path will have opened up. Connecting the human being to a prolonged immersion within the digital realms is not a 'merging' but a dissociation of the human being from their body and hence from their vehicle of sacred receptivity and transmission: it is a separation from Source. And this, as I have discussed throughout the book, is the play of the Inversion—a state of dislocation. And within this displacement, we shall be playing in the disenchanted underbelly of dark Gnosticism.

A gnostic underbelly

We may be led to believe that the Metaverse is an agnostic space, yet the covert truth is that it is a deeply dark gnostic realm where the entropic forces of materialism create a deadly enchantment. Similar to the gnostic vision of writer Philip K. Dick (see Chapter 3), the creator of the pseudo-realm is the false god/Demiurge that he refers to as an 'artefact'. Such a creative artefact constructs an artificial reality—a projected world—that is 'ruthlessly deterministic and mechanical'.[6] For the Gnostics, the material world was intrinsically evil, and the task of humanity was to escape it. There may be those people who will argue that the Metaverse is not part of the material world because it is primarily digital—yet this is a fallacy. As mentioned above, this is the trick of pulling the wool over our eyes through a reterritorialising of materiality. The Metaverse is a deeper layer within the dreaming of the material world. Just as in the film *Inception* (2010), where the protagonists are taken into progressively deeper layers of the dream world, so too is the Metaverse a deeper layer within an artificial world constructed from the material configurations of computer technology. And within the reality construct of the Metaverse, it is likely to be difficult to discern the control agendas and techniques that are part of the Demiurge—the artefact of error and falsity. Human consciousness will be redirected through distraction into a realm of extended lesser reality, and further away from both the natural world and from perception of the Greater Reality. In other words, consciousness will be monitored, stimulated, and influenced by incorporation into the meta-corporate world. We might as well get this branded now as *Consciousness Incorporated* (Meta Inc.). Creative imagination is the realm of human potential; it is what stimulates visionary ideas, innovation, and inspirational development. Yet when the human imagination is fed by data inputs, selected information, and arranged artefacts—the 'choice architecture' of behaviour control—then this forms *dense imagination*. According to Rudolf Steiner, densified imaginations are not visionary in character because they have been made heavy by an earthly materiality. They are more likely to correspond to devolutionary, entropic influences—spirits of materialism—which are dark powers that Steiner refers to as Ahrimanic forces.[7] Furthermore, dense imagination and the deterritorialisation of self leads to the loss of personal willpower and genuine intention. The capacity for focused will and intention are crucial aspects of a free and sovereign individual. And if a person does not utilise their own capacities and powers, then there will be others who shall exploit them for their own uses. The self-control and exercise of will is fundamental to humanity's development.

The acceleration towards AI constructed worlds with their techno-infrastructures is an acceleration away from human evolvement toward Source consciousness. This is the polarity, the dichotomy, that is also playing out within the Inversion through the theme of transhumanism. The materialism fallacy is that the continuing encapsulation of the human being into artificial constructs is a deepening deception of materiality. And deepening immersion into materialism is what Gnosticism essentially warns us against. In the context here, to dematerialise away from the body is not a path away from materiality but a further transgression into the containment field of artificial constructs. The crippled hero of *Avatar* (2009) displayed the imperfect nature of human physical bodies, and the need for transmigration into other bodily forms. This transhumanist cocktail is one of the purest aspects of concentrated materialism. And through this comes a profound and deadly dispiriting. In a post-pandemic world, where life is lived through Zoom, we are being thrust into a time where human-to-human contact is being replaced with interaction through technology. We are being tempted through our digital exoskeleton to embrace a new opulent gnostic realm. This is a realm where the Metaverse masquerades as the new fashion, and the Demiurge-artefact is the fashion designer. Over time, a new godlike digital space could be formed where people become their own gods, dressed as lustrous super-potent avatars, whilst their biological nervous system gets rewired to leave the human body behind. Through this will be created the greatest tech-elite dream of separation and alienation from any genuine transcendental impulses. The Inversion is a dream of disconnection; of having no direct contact with the Source of our being—with Origin. And this is the nature of the counterfeit mirror world of the Metaverse. And with the Metaverse, we become entangled in a deadly enchantment. This is the power of the Inversion.

Deadly enchantment

The current existential uncertainties and insecurities of material life are being used as a springboard to persuade people into accepting a dislocation from physical form (which is ultimately a deterritorialisation and loss of self). Through such material conditioning and indoctrination, a mechanical element is introduced which drives out the factor of extradimensional reality perception. Natural human evolvement that aims to connect the higher functions of the mind with the Greater Reality will become dampened and greatly diminished—or even eliminated altogether. Any genuine future for the human being must surely be aligned with a developmental impulse that serves to maintain correspondence with a transcendent reality beyond form. And the Metaverse will only increasingly distance people from this. This offering of a digital utopia is a strategy of sabotage in disguise. Through enchantment, the human being is being further captured into an artificial, deceptive construct. It will be this space where the cosmological contestation, between a natural evolutionary trajectory and an artificial devolutionary path, will take place. The further submersion into the electro-digital realms of the Inversion will not only create a soulful dislocation but also contribute to a potentially permanent lostness within the inner homeland of the human being. And this brings us to the subject of what fuels, or runs through, the machinic impulse: electricity.

One of the most world-changing technological discoveries of our recent era has been that of electricity. The word electricity first entered the English language in a 1650 translation of a treatise on the healing properties of magnets by Jan Baptist van Helmont, a Flemish physician and Rosicrucian who worked on the borderline between natural magic and modern chemistry. Many of the earliest books and treatises on electricity described the force in distinctly alchemical terms, with such names as the 'ethereal fire', the 'quintessential fire', or the 'desideratum', being used. Now it is taken for granted how almost everything we use today is plugged into some invisible power grid. We take little or no notice of how our devices and household appliances produce electromagnetic fields that mesh with all the other unseen fields into an ecosystem of electro-energies. These energies are sub-nature. They are part of living existence, yet they are a lower form of life vibration. Electricity, said Rudolf Steiner, is light in a *sub-material* state. That is, it is a form of light that has fallen below the level of nature and has become what he termed 'sub-nature'. It is because of this that Steiner warned humankind to be cautious not to build cultures dependent or based on electricity. An electro-ecosystem will only serve to draw us away from our natural ecosystem and into a lower vibrational state of sub-nature. In a lecture from 1925, Steiner says:

> There are very few as yet who even feel the greatness of the spiritual tasks approaching man in this direction. Electricity, for instance, celebrated since its discovery as the very soul of Nature's existence, must be recognised in its true character—in its peculiar power of leading down from Nature to Sub Nature. Only man himself must beware lest he slide downward with it.[8]

Rudolf Steiner made great efforts to outline aspects of the various forces acting against humankind's development. One of these forces he termed as 'Luciferic', and the aim of these forces was to sever the connection between the human world and the realm of spirit. The other forces he named as 'Ahrimanic', and the intention of these forces was to draw humanity into their realm; that is, to drag human beings further into deep material entanglement.

What makes Steiner's observation central to this exploration of the Inversion is that he was perhaps the first figure (spiritual researcher) to publicly refer to electricity as sub-nature, and of its possible relation to entropic (negative) forces. Specifically, how anti-developmental impulses (Ahrimanic) are connected with the forces of generated electricity and magnetism; these are the same energy processes that information/computing technologies are based upon. As electricity, light is highly compressed into a sub-material construct. The inner qualities of natural light are distorted into an artificial form below that of its original state. And from this, human technologies are created; technology utilises natural energies condensed into sub-natural—i.e. artificial—states. According to Anthroposophical researcher Paul Emberson:

> In a nutshell: technology is that sphere of human activity in which we are transforming the substances and forces of the outer mineral

world, giving them new structures, motion, properties and purposes, in accordance with our ideas, our intentions and the destiny
of our race.[9]

Through technology the human being is externalising its own nature,
manifesting an expression in material creations. Such outer creations
can be seen as projections of a person's own nature. The shifts to occur in
technology will be reflections of the changes occurring in human beings
themselves. Yet since the human being is caught up within the Inversion, becoming ever more entangled within physical matter, such technological creations ('expressions') will not come from a place of pure
consciousness. Current technological developments and processes are
not only an expression of our wishes and desires—the human ego—but
are also expressions of a machinic impulse that runs through humanity
via their embodiment in this Inversion reality. That is, forces which
operate within the Inversion are able to find expression through the
medium of technology because such technologies are outer creations of
a humanity through which such forces also operate.

Technology is also an intermediary medium through which humanity can access and interact with other forces and realities. If we exam-
ine some of the most recent technological innovations, we can see that
there is a marked potential for doing more than processing operations
within this current reality. As an example, quantum computing utilises
the properties of quantum states. According to the quantum sciences,
the phenomena of entanglement, superposition, and the particle-wave
duality concept, demonstrate a correspondence with an underlying quantum vacuum, or quantum unified field. Such a unified field
is also related to the zero-point field from which matter-reality manifests. In other words, quantum science connects with an energetic realm
beyond spacetime. Within such a realm, other dimensions, other realities exist; many quantum scientists are cognisant of this potential. David
Deutsch, a British physicist and pioneer in the field of quantum physics,
stated in 2005: 'Quantum computation … will be the first technology
that allows useful tasks to be performed in collaboration between parallel universes'.[10] Similarly, Geordie Rose, the founder of D-Wave Systems
that created the D-Wave Quantum Computer, stated in a similar talk:

> Science has reached the point now where we can build machines
> that can exploit those other worlds … The shadows of these parallel
> worlds overlap with ours and if we are smart enough, we can dive

into them and grab their resources and pull them back into ours, to make an effect in our world.[11]

Later on, Geordie Rose confessed that when standing next to his quantum computer, 'it feels like an altar to an alien God'. Yet how is a person able to distinguish between an 'alien God' and a demon—humanity has been riddled with this dilemma for millennia. Around the same time, in 2014, Tesla chief executive Elon Musk was warning of the dangers and high risks of advanced technology, such as artificial intelligence. He famously stated that 'With artificial intelligence we are summoning the demon. In all those stories where there's the guy with the pentagram and the holy water, it's like, yeah, he's sure he can control the demon. Didn't work out'.[12] As one more example from many, we can point to the large hydron collider at the European Organization for Nuclear Research (known as CERN) which many have suggested could be a means for accessing other dimensions. In a briefing to reporters, Sergio Bertolucci, who is Director for Research and Scientific Computing at CERN, stated: 'Out of this door might come something, or we might send something through it'.[13]

The pattern emerging here is that through technology, humanity is opening up the possibility of establishing correspondences with other forces and other realms. However, the inner state of the human being needs to be taken into account here for we are not dealing with external events alone. And when humanity's lower nature is in contact with (attracted to?) those forces beyond the present physical reality, then a detrimental relationship can be brought into manifestation. As has been stated within the occult sciences, it is more often the lower nature of the human being that is sought out, for alliance and unhealthy bonding.

Humanity is now coming face-to-face with technologies that transcend the known boundaries of physical space and time. These technologies are not being introduced into a vacuum, but into a matter-reality populated by predominantly carbon-based life forms through which conscious and unconscious energies flow. As yet, there is not only no real understanding of the effects on the biological nervous system and human consciousness; there is no comprehension of the impact this will have upon the inner development of humankind. The great challenge facing humanity as it steps into the future is how to manage its relationship, and increasing merger, with technology; especially in regard to the presence of the *machinic impulse*. What is clear is that for Steiner, and his fellow spiritual-science researchers, these new technologies have tremendous metaphysical weight attached to them. Furthermore, the potential negativity that such technology, and their forces, visit upon humanity may be absolutely necessary for humankind's continued development. Why this might be so is explored in the following chapter.

Notes

1. See Jean-François Lyotard's *The Postmodern Condition: A Report on Knowledge* (1979).
2. *Snow Crash* is a science fiction novel by Neal Stephenson, first published in 1992.
3. www.matthewball.vc/all/forwardtothemetaverseprimer
4. www.thelastamericanvagabond.com/great-narrative-metaverse-part-2-will-metaverse-end-human-freedom/
5. An alternative off-on world scenario was presented in the film *Elysium* (2013).
6. Philip K. Dick, 'Cosmogeny and Cosmology', in *The Shifting Realities of Philip K. Dick: Selected Literary and Philosophical Writings*, ed. Lawrence Sutin (New York: Vintage Books, 1995).
7. See 'The Occult Movement in the Nineteenth Century'—https://wn.rsarchive.org/Lectures/GA254/English/RSP1973/19151018p01.html
8. Rudolf Steiner, 'From Nature to Sub-Nature', *Anthroposophical Leading Thoughts*—https://wn.rsarchive.org/Books/GA026/English/RSP1973/GA026_c29.html.
9. Paul Emberson, *Machines and the Human Spirit* (Scotland: The DewCross Centre for Moral Technology, 2013), 12.
10. Spoken at a 2005 Ted Talk.
11. Spoken at a 2015 talk at Ideacity—https://youtu.be/PqN_2jDVbOU
12. www.washingtonpost.com/news/innovations/wp/2014/10/24/elon-musk-with-artificial-intelligence-we-are-summoning-the-demon/
13. www.theregister.com/2009/11/06/lhc_dimensional_portals/

CHAPTER 10

Stagnated evolvement
(the influence of entropic forces)

The materialistic physicians will be entrusted with the task of expelling the souls from mankind.
—Rudolf Steiner, Lecture given on 7 October 1917

Do not fear those who can kill the body but not soul. Rather be afraid of him who can destroy both soul and body in the life after death.
—Gospel of Matthew (10–28)

So far, I have introduced the machinic impulse as a force that is accelerating the automation of the human being and of life upon this planet. The machinic impulse equates to the forces of materialism. These material forces propagate an impulse and influence that if taken beyond its necessary function can lead to entropy and decay. Materialism is all good and well—yet up to a certain point. This is recognised by some as the 'Fall'—the deep immersion into physical reality. To a certain degree, this immersion into physicality was necessary for developing individualisation and to perceive existence in relation to Source. Once this recognition is gained, then begins the 'return journey' back to Source/Origin consciousness. However, if a species remains too long within the grip of materialistic forces, then a hardening—or *deadening*—can occur that crystallises certain faculties and organs of perception, which leads to an evolutionary stagnation. As such, the stagnation of evolvement can be due to the over-influence of entropic forces. The philosopher Rudolf Steiner, in his spiritual science, referred to these entropic forces as the Ahrimanic impulse. For the purpose of this chapter, I shall make reference often to this Ahrimanic impulse (or the forces of Ahriman) as a way of conceptualising energies of decay, deterioration, and decline.

The entropic forces that exist in opposition aim to 'over-materialise' materialism. They intend to deepen the entanglement within physical matter, and to create artificial material forms that would not have arisen in the natural course of human evolvement. This is a matter of exercising certain powers upon the physical plane. This is being applied in such a way as to block a renewal of human culture beyond the present age and to direct it into a new form of materialism, a more etheric form that seems un-material (or de-solidified). That is, the digital-virtual realms, whilst seeming contrary to physical-materialism, are in fact working to deepen human entanglement in material forces. As mentioned in a previous chapter, the *material fallacy* is that the digital realm and its extension into augmented reality, and into such spaces as the Metaverse, is a further deepening into materialism rather than a release from it. These digitised spaces, because of their sense of non-physicality, are really an etheric manifestation of materialism. Or rather, a realm of theoretical materialism (also a Steiner term). Theoretical materialism signifies a reality construct that does not need to be physical to the touch, yet it is based on, or is a projection from, a material foundation. Within both the theoretical and regular mode of materialism, the human being is encapsulated within an amalgamation of material processes. It is also a world of facts and external evidence that a person becomes lost within. All life experience proceeds from this material realm, and this conditions the human being to gain a view of life that is factually based, and to accept that there is no other reality except this world of materialism and factual experience. Any notion of the soul or spirit—the transcendental impulse—is either regarded as being a by-product of material reality or is rejected altogether as a false notion. This is the power of the immersion into matter-reality.

Deep materialism finally becomes a cosmology of entropy and decline. It leads to mechanical, artificial modes of thinking that eventually bring about a stagnation in those forces driving human development. If continued, these materialistic forces—the machinic impulse—carve out a path of technological advancement and evolution that further blocks vital, spiritualised forces. In this route, the human being strives for greater material benefits yet neglects the vital human forces of spiritualised connection. According to Steiner, our current epoch is the one which is concerned with the development of the material world; and if the human being is not to degenerate totally into a mere accomplice of machines, then a path must be found which leads from the mechanical impulse towards a life of the spirit. However, entropic forces are in play that are opposed to forms of 'spiritualisation' (inner freedom), and which work to reduce and, eventually, dispose of internal development and to replace it with an ethereal and otherworldly 'virtual paradise' where all needs can be fulfilled-by-illusion. A part of this 'hyper-materialism' is the notion of immortality that is arising through transhumanist tropes. This can be referred to as *Ahrimanic immortality* as it works not through the spirit-soul but through a prolongation of the physical life experience by merger with machinic forms. This is a mode of potential immortality within the physical sphere but not within the metaphysical. In the end, it is an entrapment for it disavows the inner spirit release from the physical domain. This can lead to a state of soullessness within the human being as the contact with Source becomes, over time, diminished. Or, perhaps this materialistic, transhumanist agenda will attract those people already without full spirit-soul incarnation.

It may be that there are people walking around in physical incarnation, in physical bodies, yet who are lacking, for want of a better word, a *soul*. Rudolf Steiner made note of this a hundred years ago when he stated:

> a kind of surplus of individuals is appearing in our times who are without Egos ['I'], who are not truly human beings. This is a terrible truth ... They make the impression of a human being if we do not look closely, but they are not human in the fullest sense of the word.[1]

Steiner warned us to be aware that what we encounter as human beings in human form may not always have to be what it appears to be. He stated that the outer appearance can be just that: appearance. He went on to state:

> We encounter people in human form who only in their outer appearance are individuals ... in truth, these are humans with a

> physical, etheric, and astral body, but beings are embodied in them, beings that make use of these individuals in order to operate through them.[2]

What this refers to is that human bodies can be vessels for other beings to operate through.

This makes us realise that the world of 'spirit'—or the occult—may not always be what we have thought it to be, for there are players and forces that wield a great deal of influence within the physical world. And some of these influences act through the presence of certain individuals that may appear outwardly 'normal'. In this light, a completely different kind of spirituality is at work in present-day humanity—and this is what I have repeatedly referred to as the Inversion. It can be understood from this that certain power groups, and their individual members, are influenced (and perhaps dominated) by a non-human species of being (entropic forces) that are intent on implementing non-human objectives. Such groups and individuals would, in this case, exhibit a distinct lack of 'soul'—i.e. empathy and compassion—and would appear to others as displaying almost sociopathic tendencies. Yet at the same time, such people can appear unusually charismatic and are able to exert great influence over other people, especially with their words and speeches, whilst being themselves emotionally stunted. If we take only a cursory glance at the actions of many incumbent leaders, politicians, corporate businesses, financial institutions, and more, we can see a clear lack of any soulful behaviour or intent. Quite the contrary, many of these individuals and groups seem determined to curtail human freedoms, sovereignty, and inner empowerment. If Steiner were alive today, he would no doubt say that what we are currently witnessing upon the physical plane is an act of soulless terraforming of the planet and a controlling manipulation of the human life experience by nefarious forces that have anti-human aims and intentions.

Furthermore, such beings might be motivated in their actions to attempt to block other human being's connection to their own individual inner/spiritual impulse. By a range of actions, they could focus on distracting people away from the notion of a metaphysical reality and of their inherent connection to Source (or a realm of vital conscious intelligence beyond matter-reality). In extreme cases, such players might even target the bio-psycho human body in an attempt to sabotage the vessel so as to make it a less viable vehicle for soul-spirit incarnation.

What else might they hope to achieve? Again, referring to Rudolf Steiner, he stated that:

> Their objective is to maintain the whole of life as a mere economic life, to gradually eradicate everything else that is part of the intellectual and spiritual life, to eradicate the spiritual life precisely where it is most active ... and swallow up everything through the economic life.[3]

These entropic forces, which Steiner calls Ahrimanic forces, distract humanity from aligning with its evolutionary potential and developmental source by introducing mechanisms and processes of stagnation and decay. To accomplish this, a specific materialistic and mechanical construct of life is established based on rational-materialistic and scientific dogma. This is the impulse that now permeates the current mode of the Inversion. Our lesser reality has become inverted into a territory that is acclimatised for Ahrimanic, entropic forces.

To give more description of this 'Ahrimanic environment', it is one that cultivates antagonistic nationalisms and frictions over divided ethnicity and racial identities; polarised party politics and political tensions; the subjugation of cultural life to economic power; the mechanisation of industry and modern life; cultural censorship and manufactured political correctness; identity confusions; social division and the breakdown of social alliances; industrialised and corporate healthcare; scientific statistics and empirical data; corporate profit-seeking and powerful corporate interests; the increasing automation and artificiality of human life; economic domination; the negation of all genuine spiritual traditions; the rise of technocracy and technocratic forms of governance; the increasing social management and surveillance of the populations; the standardisation of entertainment and cultural events; the dominant worldview of mechanisation over the organic; increased immorality; the loss of value and tradition; and so much more. Steiner was also explicit in stating that the most dangerous aspect of Ahriman is for this presence to go unrecognised for it seeks to be hidden. He added: 'think of everything that presses us down upon the earth, that makes us dull and philistine, leading us to develop materialistic attitudes, penetrating us with a dry intellect, and so on: there you have a picture of Ahrimanic powers'.[4] For many, such materialistic progress appears contrary to notions of stagnation and decay. And this is where the sly, and dry, intelligence of entropic forces show their strength. Such 'Ahrimanic forces' aim to block evolvement by stimulating a particular form of progress; that is, by accelerating all modes of mechanical processes. We can see this if we only take a brief look at events today: almost everything is 24/7 full-on access; continuous distractions through online devices; short-term projects; the push for quick results, etc. Ahrimanic forces organise this acceleration deliberately so as to prevent the human being from developing and maturing their inner self, and to block people from reaching a fully conscious relationship with developmental impulses. These forces are shaping superficial people, without an inner world, who act and think automatically and align with a mechanically minded society.

What is occurring here is a deliberate push to accelerate matters before their time. This will then create further imbalance. Individual freedom and inner-life autonomy is part of humanity's innate heritage; however, opposing forces will act to frustrate, slow down, and even block human development. An aspect of these forces acts through illusions and dream fantasies (Metaverse), whilst others aim to push humanity into deeper materialism (automation—transhumanism). In this mix, we see the empty fantasy meshed with the automated mind. The destination for such entropic forces is for a dark, materialistic culture. Within this deeply materialistic culture, all traces of free, individualised humans will be targeted and eroded. The aim here is to divert the human being from developing an individualised consciousness and to steer people into docile masses—a form of pseudo-humanity. These forces can also be said to represent humanity's lower nature— as expressed selfishly through commercial-consumerist cultures, filled with superficial personalities. It is the outward gaze that seeks material pursuits, and which denies the inner spirit and expansive consciousness. Those people deeply embedded within materialism display an 'Ahrimanic consciousness'. Social forms of individualisation are instead the behaviour of selfish, individualistic drives. The rise of such entropic forces in our societies shows itself through the increasing popularity of empty words. Deep communication gets hijacked into emoticons, abbreviated words, short text messages, slogans, and twitterings. Words and language become subsumed by subconscious forces, and people are increasingly oblivious to this. As it is said, the demons of materialism speak through empty words.

At the same time, it needs to be recognised that this is the current state of the Inversion reality, and it is a phase that has to be worked through. We cannot avoid the fact that we have to learn first how to live amongst these entropic forces before we can bypass them—for these are the conditions of our time. Yet we must find the right way to approach these forces without being overpowered or subsumed by them. What may be needed to counteract Ahrimanic forces is perseverance and consistency—a long-term aim and development. We need to be aware that the forces acting against us intend to steer human intelligence into mere intellectual cleverness, driven by lower passions and desires, and increasingly divorced from a transcendental, metaphysical reality. This is the ideal vehicle for entropic forces—a pure, dry, and mechanical intellect. And if this cannot be achieved successfully through current humanity, then it will be attempted through the machinic, or robotic, path of development. And this is what connects these forces with the artificial light of electricity.

Let there be light

In the previous chapter it was introduced that Rudolf Steiner considered electricity to be a force of sub-nature, and thus corresponding to entropic (negative) forces. Steiner stated that anti-developmental impulses (what he calls Ahrimanic) are connected with the forces of human-generated electricity, which are the same energy processes that much of our technologies are based upon. He stated that:

> We must be quite clear about this: in the days when there were no electric currents, when there were no electric wires buzzing in the air, it was easier to be human. In those days these Ahrimanic forces were not there, constantly robbing us of our body even when we are awake. It was not necessary then for people to make such efforts in order to approach the spirit. That is why it is necessary today to muster far stronger spiritual forces merely to remain human than it was a hundred years ago.[5]

This warning for people to make efforts to approach the spirit was given a hundred years ago; how much further humanity now finds itself enmeshed within mechanical forces today. These entropic forces, we are told, find a means of entry into this dimension through electricity, which is decaying light. A mechanistic infrastructure could thus serve as a vehicle—a 'body'—for these non-human forces. Similarly, in Arabic and Islamic culture the concept of the djinn as an evil spirit is well recognised. So much so, that mention of the power and malevolence of the djinns is mentioned several times through the Islamic holy book, the Quran. In the history of djinns, they are often referred to as beings of 'smokeless fire', which in modern terms might easily equate with electrical beings. Such beings or forces, whether evil, Ahrimanic, or djinn, appear to have a binding towards a form of atomised technology—i.e. technology fuelled by the motion of atoms—and this should give us a note of caution since modern life is fast becoming all-electrified.

A technical, and technological, civilisation would prove to be an ideal realm for such entropic forces to have their dominion, and from where they would operate to counteract the developmental impulses of human evolvement. Again, stating Steiner on this matter:

> But in the age of technical science hitherto, the possibility of finding a true relationship to the Ahrimanic civilization has escaped man. He must find the strength, the inner force of knowledge, in order not to be overcome by Ahriman in this technical civilization. He must understand sub-nature for what it really is. This he can only do if he rises, in spiritual knowledge, at least as far into extra-earthly super-nature as he has descended, in technical science, into sub-nature. The age requires a knowledge transcending nature, because in its inner life it must come to grips with a life-content which has sunk far beneath nature—a life-content whose influence is perilous ...[6]

Steiner is compelling us to develop our understanding of spiritual matters so as to not fall prey to these sub-natural forces that have increased their presence within this technical phase of humanity's development. Why, we may ask, are these forces so prevalent from the early 20th century onwards? Somewhat coincidentally, or in correspondence, Steiner indicated the year 1879 as the moment when certain negative forces were expulsed from their dimension and entered into Earth's lesser reality (and hence into the Inversion). If we take a closer look at the year of 1879, we also find that Thomas Edison, who invented electric power generation, filed his patent for the electric lamp on 4 November

1879 (US patent 223,898), and which was granted on 27 January 1880. Edison had made the first public demonstration of his incandescent light bulb on 31 December 1879, in Menlo Park. And artificial light, we are told, carries the negative impulse of the Ahrimanic, entropic forces.

Steiner also revealed the occult fact that, since the year 1879, the human ethereal body is becoming less closely bound to the physical body, thus opening the possibility of new faculties of perception, such as psychic powers. However, this capacity and potential is being blocked by counteracting forces, especially through the use of fear and insecurity. Within the current state of the Inversion, it appears that there are negative forces attempting to infiltrate the human body at the same time that they are seeking to find expression through the machinic ecosystem. Furthermore, there is some speculation that increased materialism in physical life hardens the ethereal body so that it does not dissolve after death but remains near the Earth for a longer time. This ethereal body could serve as a vehicle, or host, for such Ahrimanic forces so that these soulless sheaths remain permanently tied to the earthly dimension and cannot move on. That is, entities can find 'bodies'—or a home—for them to remain an influence over this dimension. This state of affairs could be mirrored upon the Earth through transhumanism if physical bodies are disallowed to die completely, thus providing a host body for these entities, directly within the physical, material realm. It would seem that an artificial world, or realm, is in development—i.e. our current world is being terraformed—to accommodate such forces that are less amenable to a carbon, organic environment. It certainly causes a pause for reflection when we look out upon a world being chastised for its copious amounts of carbon, and the current zealous drives towards a carbon-zero future.

If this agenda for a complete mechanical-material domain was ever achieved, then developmental Source impulses could become cut off from human evolution. The purely Ahrimanic would dominate this sphere. With this in mind, it can be recognised how the advancing mechanisation of human civilisation is under an Ahrimanic influence. As Rudolf Steiner once commented: 'Humanity is facing a destiny where the body may be filled with Ahrimanic demonic powers'.[7] The ongoing destruction of the natural, organic world opens itself up for a replacement by Ahrimanic entropic forces, where a machinic civilisation (based on the machinic impulse) would construct a wholly new technocratic, automated realm. When the ecosystems of nature are broken down, reduced to material systems, then the building blocks for artificial structures—structures devoid of life—are established which give host for the incarnation and expression of anti-evolutionary beings and forces. This would eventually produce a whole new realm of existence.

The present times are hyper-materialistic and heavily intellect dominant. This creates an enslavement of human thinking where free speech, human imagination, and intuition, are highly controlled and subjected to monitoring, management, and technocratic administration. If this continues then it is likely to lead to a state where the human species, unknowing to itself, will have lost the ability for true, genuine thinking. The inner world will have become diminished, and any developmental impulses are over-ridden by material forces. The Inversion will have completed its full reversal from the realm of Higher Truth. This compels those aware individuals during these times to maintain the connection between the transcendental realm and the physical world. There must be a correspondence alive, and maintained, within the earthly realm at all times. This is the lifeline that allows for the developmental forces to operate within the physical sphere through materiality itself. The only way to move through these times is by humanity confronting the entropic forces whilst being in the world, by overcoming and transforming them.

The times are near at hand where human beings will once again have access to psychic abilities—such as clairvoyance—that was once a part of their natural inheritance. It will again come about as part of humanity's natural development. Yet the Ahrimanic forces are working to divert this by pushing humanity further into deep materialism. The signs of this will be a rise in intellectual pseudo-thinking, falsity, pseudo-truths, and the loss of discernment. The pervasiveness of entropic forces will work towards blocking humankind's evolvement, and to steer this into a route of evolutionary stagnation. Human intelligence will be appropriated, taken away, and placed into automated systems so that the muscles of human thought and imagination will atrophy over time. Without the vital forces of the human spirit, the mechanical impulse will remain immoral and unethical. It will continue to function, yet without *being*. Without an interpenetration of the mechanical and the moral—matter and spirit—future development in this domain will split.

It is the responsibility of those aware individuals today to make sure that this splitting does not occur. Instead, an alchemical operation of grand proportions must take place. The infiltration and penetration of entropic forces in this reality does not necessarily have to be a negative event. Forces are corrective upon both sides: as there is a push, so there is a pull. And the pull can be from within the individual. If we recognise that the intervention of entropic forces in human life are a necessary trigger for developing our own intention and conscious evolvement, then we can utilise these events to our advantage. It is through resistance to the counterforces against evolvement where humanity finds its strength for freedom. The question is whether we can meet these challenges in the right way.

Notes

1. Cited in Erdmuth Johannes Grosse, *Are There People Without A Self?* (Forest Row: Temple Lodge, 2021), 31–32.
2. Cited in Erdmuth Johannes Grosse, *Are There People Without A Self?* (Forest Row: Temple Lodge, 2021), 60.
3. Cited in Erdmuth Johannes Grosse, *Are There People Without A Self?* (Forest Row: Temple Lodge, 2021), 63.
4. Rudolf Steiner, *The Incarnation of Ahriman: The Embodiment of Evil on Earth* (Forest Row: Rudolf Steiner Press, 2009), 1.
5. Rudolf Steiner, 'Concerning Electricity'. A lecture given in Dornach, 28 January 1923 (GA 220).
6. Rudolf Steiner, 'From Nature to Sub-Nature', in *Anthroposophical Leading Thoughts*, trans. George and Mary Adams (London: Rudolf Steiner Press, 1973).
7. Rudolf Steiner, *The Incarnation of Ahriman: The Embodiment of Evil on Earth* (Forest Row: Rudolf Steiner Press, 2009).

CHAPTER 11

Incarnations
(or the hybrid self)

Where there is bright light, there are deep shadows.

—Old Saying

Humanity had to go to sleep spiritually so that spirituality could reappear in a new form.

—Rudolf Steiner

People nowadays allow themselves to be too easily offended by information that they consider to be outside their remit. It is also increasingly difficult in these times to speak of truthful matters, especially in concern of the spirit-consciousness, for people are inculcated with false beliefs and thinking patterns. This is itself a sign of social conditioning and of a certain 'management of mind'. We should not be surprised that this situation is rife throughout our human societies and is becoming increasingly predominant. Social norms are persuading many people to prefer safety and security rather than the potential discomfort that comes from genuine realisation. A perceptive understanding of the human condition recognises that inner potentials lie within our creative imagination. This is the true realm that allows for Source expression within the physical domain. Yet, unfortunately, we have seen within the pages of this book how the Inversion has usurped this into a construct of fantasy, make-believe, and the crass and superficial culture industries that rule over these lands. Any notion of Higher or Greater Reality has been twisted into an artificial lesser reality that serves to block, as far as is possible, the developmental impulse from penetrating. This arrangement has culminated in dissociating humankind not only from its natural, organic, carbon-based environment, but also from its inherent contact with its origin—Source consciousness. This increasing disembodiment is reflected in such forms as the techno-digital ecosystem, extended reality, computerisation (including algorithms), and artificial intelligence. For many people today, their digital devices have become their instruments of false salvation (i.e. enslavement).

A recognition and resurrection of the inner life of the human being is now of paramount importance. This is the window of time, of opportunity, as humanity finds itself fraught with uncertainties and many unwelcome forces. What is required is nothing less than a human re-evolutionary revival from lower impulses and stunted understanding towards a fuller realisation of self. This is time for a 'reckoning' with oneself, for there to be any chance of developing our innate human higher faculties from within the Inversion. This is not a time for drawing back and retreating into one's inner cave of darkness and ignorance, like an individualised expression of the medieval ages. Collective ignorance was a state that had to be passed through for there to be a stepping into an individualised self-awareness. A period of 'inner sleeping' has enabled humanity to be in a position to regain its spirit-consciousness faculties as if anew. And abstract truths were dominant so as to force people to reach forth for more recognisable inner truths. Modernity was arrived at through this period of gradual individual awakening from a slumber of mass formation, or mass-conditioned mentality. To remain at this level would be disastrous for human development, for it would indicate a falling back into lower states of vibration based upon base instincts and appetites. It would also lead to opening the door towards further, and much increased, domination and enslavement. What is needed is for a significant number of individuals to recognise the inner tools and capacities they already possess, and to relate to these. To quote again from Rudolf Steiner:

> Humanity needs to take up that which flows down from the spiritual heights into earthly life. It can be rejected. If it is rejected there

then ceases for those people who have rejected it the possibility of
human progress, of cultural progress, of human civilization, and
the further development of humanity will have to be sought among
other peoples, and in other areas ...[1]

To reiterate, humanity now needs to take up that which is flowing
'down from the spiritual heights into earthly life'. It can be rejected, as
Steiner notes; yet if it is rejected, then there is the consequence that those
people who have rejected it lose the possibility for their further development. And in this, they also hinder the progress of human civilisation
as a whole. This may sound dramatic, yet we need also to recognise
what is at stake in these times.

The more we close ourselves off by losing ourselves in materiality,
the more we are in danger of calibrating our lives in alignment with the
machinic impulse, and to a mode of automation. This then clears the
path towards transhumanism, technocracy, and the domination of entropic forces, as previously mentioned. A closed-down person is an ideal
candidate for inclusion into a socially managed and mind-programmed
mass. This must be seen now for these forces and impulses are present in the Inversion with increasing speed and ferocity. It is imperative
that we do not get caught up within a mesh of materialism that supplies many fantasies and promises, yet ultimately delivers a package
of containment, control, and even possession. We need to recognise, in
order to inform ourselves, that there are power groups operating within
the Inversion (with the knowledge that they are participating in the
Inversion), who deliberately create programming, narratives, events,
and more, that deepen the engulfing materialism. This is with the aim
of steering (i.e. social managing) the majority of humanity to believe
wholeheartedly in the dominance of materialistic forces. These groups
want to ensure that the masses live and breathe materialistic thoughts,
at the exclusion of metaphysical thinking, from their birth until death
(from the womb to the tomb). This deliberate push into a deepened
materialistic path—the extension of reality into the digital realms of
etheric materialism (as discussed in Chapter 9)—not only denies the
existence of the spirit but attempts to imprison this vital force within a
cage of electrified matter.

This makes the current task for humanity right now a more difficult
one, for such entropic anti-evolutionary forces must be recognised and
confronted—and then, transformed into positive impulses for human

development. This is all the more difficult at this time for there are also influences in place to push people into a space of 'personal darkening' that aims to debilitate, entrap, and block individual sovereignty and empowerment. The impact and consequences of the incoming forces and impulses very much depend upon the state of consciousness with which they are met. And this will determine how humanity progresses, and whether it develops in evolutionary alignment or not. World forces, both those operating within visibility and those non-visibly, would prefer that humanity resides in a state of unknowing. To this end, it is our present responsibility to strive to be more and more conscious, and to stimulate conscious awareness in as many people as possible. It is no longer a long-term feasibility to remain in ignorance of the aims behind world affairs, or the processes that target people's beliefs and thinking patterns. Similarly, to be absent of the transcendental impulse in our lives is ultimately a path to stagnation in terms of inner development. As a species, we either evolve and develop, or we do not. And the evolvement of the human species entails that a segment of the population become receptive to, and aware of, the cosmic impulses that connect us to realities of consciousness beyond our current realm. This knowledge needs to become more generally known and spoken about, rather than kept occult as it has been for ages past. Otherwise, the human species is in danger of succumbing to entropic influences that will work to diminish critical thinking, imaginative expression, and freedom of the life experience. As in all times, only a minority of aware and receptive individuals are needed—not a majority.

Such entropic forces are the forces of opposition regarding the inner development of humankind. And these forces have been compelled to make their move now, before enough individuals within the collective gain conscious awareness of the transcendental impulses that connect humanity with Source. This is the period of spirit-consciousness, which is why the counterforces are working desperately to act against these developmental processes. It is in this period that the conscious, individualised, independent thinking human being is required to emerge. And emerge we must: to break through the encroaching psychological web of lies, deceit, and programming. It is the programming side that is becoming increasingly dominant for it is pervasive now in forms of social conditioning and 'mind management'—literally so, as in the software programmes, algorithms, and artificial intelligences that run in the digital background of physical life. In Steiner's terms, the Ahrimanic forces are incarnating through the electrical sub-nature ecosystem in an attempt to gain control and influence over human life and thought. There are already major signs that many people have adopted a digitalisation of thought, with abbreviated texting, twitterings, and social media mutterings becoming dominant forms of everyday communication and expression. The digitalisation of human thoughts has erupted massively since the arrival of advanced computing and computer networks, although its earlier inception was with the printing press (beginning with Gutenberg) and the distribution and massification of information. In the words of the Russian thinker Sergei Prokofieff:

> It follows that the whole computer and Internet industry is today the most effective way to prepare for the imminent incarnation of Ahriman or at least to allow his earthly task to run as smoothly as possible for him. The net of Ahrimanic spider beings developing out of the internet around the earth stands right from the beginning in a direct relationship to Ahriman appearing in a physical body and will serve him particularly effectively and offer him extremely favourable potential to work.[2]

Here is a direct indication that the influence, or seduction, of Ahrimanic forces is already in play. People across the world have been connected like never before, and are communicating, organising, and informing themselves through these networks of communication. Yet the danger here, in relation to entropic forces, is that these webs of interrelation slyly coax a person deeper into the materialistic web and further away from inner connection to the metaphysical realms (including Source consciousness). Connection on the physical-digital level may increasingly denote isolation in relation to the transcendental.

As stated, the greatest danger concerning these entropic forces is if their presence, activity, and influence go unrecognised. These influences take great efforts to remain largely hidden or, at the least, beyond the perceptions of the majority. In this way, they can stealthily establish conditions that make people increasingly dependent upon their systems and within their sphere of control. The incarnation and presence of such forces is recognised also through the push toward dominance of the intellect over imagination and inner values. The intelligence of the intellect is seductive, and logically reasonable (of course), yet it negates the role of the inner vital forces and that of the metaphysical domain. If this continues into the extreme, then it will lead to a collective state of inner blindness among humankind. Anti-developmental forces seek to exercise their control through influencing both the conscious and sub-conscious minds of people by means of instilling fear: fear of well-being, security, and economic status. The focus of distraction, since the earliest years of education, is placed upon the person's lower needs—such as work, money, home, and belonging—rather than upon the forms of self-knowledge that strengthen the internal gaze and higher faculties of perception. The human being too has been colonised in an interior way through layer upon layer of misdirected education/information (or, in other words, programming). In general, people who live in this modern age of controlled media, insipient entertainment, corrupt politics, managed economies, and more, have been purposefully impacted and influenced so as to be inwardly stunted. Outward signs of physical and mental activity may easily hide a true state of inner stagnation. If the entropic forces that work to block human development become prevalent within, and through people, then a dissociation occurs that hampers further inner growth within the individual. There is no more inward maturity as the counterforces place all attention onto external, superficial projections. This is the state of a great many of our supposedly 'high status' individuals of today—including world leaders, corporate CEOs, bankers and financiers, and, especially, those high-powered people running the tech giants. The masses are being led blindly by the inwardly immature who, perhaps unknown to themselves, are vessels for the incarnating influence of entropic, Ahrimanic forces. In the end, human civilisation must choose one of two alignments—with de-evolutionary processes (leading to decay and destruction), or with the development of the spirit-consciousness of humankind.

Negative influences have already been allowed to gain too great a foothold upon the Earth. Much of this, though certainly not all of it, is due to a small minority of persons (the so-called elite) aligning themselves, through greed and power, with anti-human forces that seek to control and contain human freedom and development. Their power fuels the programmed illusions that rule over us, through our acceptance or consent, and which subsequently dominate over the world, its nations and, perhaps soon, the whole earthly realm. An alternate sphere of existence may have already incarnated.

The eighth sphere

Now here's an interesting little story that erupted in the occult world in the final years of the 19th century. In 1893, a series of lectures were given to a group of individuals who were known as the Berean Society. These lectures were given by C. G. Harrison, a deeply learned initiate, as well as a committed Christian. It turned out that Harrison had been elected to expound upon a body of information in the public realm that had hitherto remained highly secretive. Secretive, that is, until a particular breach had occurred regarding the dissemination of information kept within the guardianship of certain secret societies. This series of public lectures was the first to discuss openly the nature of the internal conflicts that had arisen between some of the Mystery Schools in 19th-century Europe and America. As Harrison explained in his opening lectures, this breach concerned the Theosophy Society, which is associated largely with the colourful and controversial character of Madame Blavatsky. Harrison referred to this breach as a conflict 'behind the veil'. The reason for such secrecy around certain forms of knowledge is that the knowledge in question, says Harrison, is 'the key to a power which would be highly dangerous to society (as at present constituted) if it were to become public property'.[3] That is, there are reasons for keeping some information away from the hands of the ignorant (for their sake as well as for others). For once a breach is made, it is harder to undo and easier to be widened.

As Harrison went on to explain, the breach, or exposure of incorrect information, was due to a publication from the high-ranking Theosophist, A. P. Sinnett, in his work *Esoteric Buddhism* (1883). Part of the information that Sinnett made public referenced the 'Eighth Sphere' and its relationship with the evolution of humanity upon the Earth. Harrison noted that Sinnett made an incorrect judgement regarding the association of the Eighth Sphere to the Earth's satellite, the Moon. This was either an error of judgement or an error of ignorance. Either way, it was considered, from certain quarters, that this now publicly made error could not go uncontested. The consequences, it had been decided, were too significant to let be. In regard to the Eighth Sphere, Harrison stated that the mystery surrounding its very nature 'is a key to the problem of evil in the Universe'.[4] He went on to say, in relation to this, that there can be a considerable danger when the lower nature of humanity is attracted to certain forces beyond the physical realm, as a harmful relationship can be brought into manifestation. It is, stated Harrison, the lower nature of the human being that is constantly being sought out, for alliance and unhealthy bonding. Whether we, as individuals, are consciously aware of this or not, there are certain energetic forces that seek to attract and form 'bonds of influence' with human beings between realms. Other sources have referred to these elements as 'hostile forces', whereas I have used the term 'entropic forces'. And such forces exist in a space not far, energetically speaking, from where we stand right now. Also, through certain amateur rituals and practices, many of which are brought into being through ignorance, these forces can gain a stronger influence over aspects of earthly existence. One 20th-century occultist (writing under the name of Mark Hedsel) referred to the Eighth Sphere as a 'shadow sphere' that was controlled by shadow beings. This realm seeks to capture and pull away what may be termed 'materialised spiritual energy' from the Earth sphere into the Eighth Sphere. This realm, the Eighth Sphere, is like a vacuum, claims Hedsel.[5] It is a realm that sucks things into its own existence, a shadowy realm. It is vibrationally and developmentally lower than the Earth's sphere. It is, according to Hedsel, a shadow sphere controlled by shadow beings—yet they can be more cunning and intelligent than humankind for they lack our conscience and compassion. These shadow beings wish to fill their realm with human souls, so they have placed portals upon the Earth that act as conduits for sucking up lower forms of spiritual energy from the Earth plane. These portals can be opened by certain rituals, as in black magic, or through naïve seances and 'spiritualist' style meetings and channelling. They wish to trap human soul-energy into their shadow realm—like a realm of the damned. These beings are similar to demons, and they counteract the evolutionary impulse within humankind. In Steiner's terminology, these can be referred to as Ahrimanic beings, and the Eighth Sphere as an abode of Ahriman.

In fact, shortly after the above 'breach' by A. P. Sinnett, Steiner himself felt forced to address the highly mysterious topic of the Eighth Sphere and to bring it out more into the open:

> It is very difficult indeed to speak about the so-called 'Eighth Sphere' which was referred to openly for the first time by Mr. Sinnett ... what is called the Eighth Sphere can have nothing directly to do with anything within the material world—that is to say, what can be perceived by man's senses and thought out on the

basis of sensory perception has no part in the Eighth Sphere. So it will be useless to look for the Eighth Sphere anywhere in the material world.[6]

Of course, the realm of the Eighth Sphere is not in the physical-material domain but operates upon a different vibration. However, it can be perceived by way of 'visionary-imaginative clairvoyance', says Steiner. Steiner discusses the existence of the Eighth Sphere in a similar way to Hedsel, yet within a more complex and cosmological framework. Whereas Hedsel refers to the Eighth Sphere as a 'shadow sphere' that is controlled by shadow beings trapping, or sucking, human soul-energy, Steiner brings it into the operations of Luciferic and Ahrimanic forces. The Eighth Sphere is a realm that counteracts the evolutionary, cosmological path of humankind. And how it works is that Luciferic and Ahrimanic forces attempt to strip from humanity certain energies—or 'mineralisations'—that then are used to energise the formation and existence of this entropic realm. As Steiner quoted in one of his lectures:

> Lucifer and Ahriman strive unceasingly to draw from the Earth's substances whatever they can snatch, in order to form their Eighth Sphere which then, when it is sufficiently advanced, will be detached from the Earth and go its own way in the Cosmos together with Lucifer and Ahriman.[7]

Here, Steiner is depicting these forces in the way of thieves; awaiting and attempting to take from humanity certain elements or, most likely, energies.

Further, Steiner's depiction of this situation is that humankind is targeted where it is most vulnerable—at its head. That is, through the intellect. Again, we come back here to the question of materialism, which is a rational, intellectual domain. This, we are told, is going on all the time around us, only that we are not aware of its happenings. The activity for the Eighth Sphere is taking place 'behind the scenes of our existence', says Steiner. We can see much of this 'behind the scenes' activity now manifesting in our modern lives as rapidly advancing material technologies—especially artificial intelligence programmes, automated algorithms, and data-infrastructures. This new material-digital ecosystem is head-based: the notion of 'programming' is itself an intellectual skill (perhaps the alternative programming community is more creative here). Steiner was very explicit in his description of this situation:

> Care had to be taken that not everything in man proceeding from the head can become the prey of Lucifer and Ahriman; that not everything shall depend upon head-activity and the activity of the outward-turned senses, for then Lucifer and Ahriman would have been victors. It was necessary that a counterweight should be created in the domain of earthly life, that there should be in the human being something entirely independent of the head. And this was achieved through the work of the good Spirits of Form, who implanted the principle of *Love* into the principle of heredity on Earth. That is to say, there is now operative in the human race something that is independent of the head, that passes from generation to generation and has its deepest foundations in the physical nature of man.[8]

The counterweight to the intellect was implanted into earthly life—the principle of *Love*. This is a highly significant remark, for it shows that evolutionary forces, working through the 'Spirits of Form', are counteracting the entropic impulses. Further, that the Love principle is both worldly as well as being beyond the world. That is, much more beyond that of only physical love. The Love impulse is a transcendental force that acts through materiality and yet is also much more besides. It is necessary for it to be operative amongst humankind, for it aligns with another significant force that the human being must acquire—freedom of the will. And this freedom of will can be acquired only during incarnation in the physical realm. Why is this?

When the human spirit is in the pre-incarnation and post-incarnation state, it regains full knowledge of its existence among the spirit realms. In this state of spirit-consciousness, all is known. However, during physical incarnation the human spirit accepts forgetfulness so that it can make its choices from a place of freedom. That is, without knowing the relationships to its existence beyond physicality. It is through these choices that life incarnations gain experiences. The freedom of will to make these life choices, and the acceptance of their consequences, are fundamental to the development of the human being. This is precisely why the entropic forces attempt to curtail free will amongst humans—a non-developmental path can then more easily be aligned with the domain of the Eighth Sphere. Because of this, influences upon the Earth are continually trying to wrestle free will away from humanity. We only have to see current life conditions around the world to see how this pattern is operative and is increasing rapidly. Steiner was very clear on this matter: 'Lucifer and Ahriman are engaged perpetually in shackling man's free will and in conjuring all sorts of things before him in order to tear away what he makes out of these things and let it disappear in the Eighth Sphere'.[9] This wrestling of free will away from the individual has entered popular mythology in the symbolism of the devil tempting, or bargaining for, the human soul (such as in Goethe's *Faust*).

The temptations on offer to the individual from these evolution-ary counterforces are varied. Another subterfuge, according to Steiner, is that these forces pretend that the Eighth Sphere is the realm of the dead—of loved ones who have passed over the veil. Through seances and mediums, people are fooled into communicating with spectres of the Eighth Sphere rather than with genuine human souls in the spirit realms. This spiritualist trap, or fallacy, reached its peak during the late 19th and early 20th century as mediums, seances, and the world of Spiritism became the fashion. The domain of the dead may very well be the realm of the shadows, and the seances are their portals—exactly as described earlier by occultist Mark Hedsel. Here we have a perfect example of how the Inversion operates; it reverses the actuality and from this conjures up a substitute reality. Steiner, amongst others, warns us that everything capable of bringing the human being/soul into con-nection with the Eighth Sphere must be rejected. Today we see that announcements of visionary clairvoyants are often greeted with won-der and awe and raised to social media celebrity status. We should be wary, and use discretion, when it comes to pseudo-spiritual announce-ments about channellings, New Age fluff, and other elements that claim to be from 'visionary clairvoyance'. It could very well be that these are aspects coming from the shadowy world of the Eighth Sphere.

Likewise, whenever people, both individually and collectively, have their freedoms curtailed, their will bent by persuasion, propaganda, or force, and their sovereign rights suppressed, then they are being steered towards the de-evolutionary realm of the Eighth Sphere. Any society that does not protect the freedom and will of the human indi-vidual is fostering a society of enslavement. And enslavement, whether through force or willing compliance, is an environment ideally suited to the domination of entropic, counter-evolutionary forces. In our times, this may be emerging through the machinic impulse and the rise of hyper-materialism, as I have endeavoured to show throughout this book. These are the forces, influences, and impulses of the Inversion—and not of Greater Reality. However, the transcendental impulses of the Greater Reality are continually permeating the lesser reality of the Inversion—and to this we now turn.

Notes

1. Rudolf Steiner, *Knowledge of the Higher Worlds* (Forest Row: Rudolf Steiner Press, 2011).
2. Sergei Prokofieff, 'The Being Of The Internet', https://philosophyof-freedom.com/the-being-of-the-internet (accessed 31 August 2022).
3. C. G. Harrison, *The Transcendental Universe* (London: Azafran Books, 2021), 21.
4. C. G. Harrison, *The Transcendental Universe* (London: Azafran Books, 2021), 88.
5. Mark Hedsel, *The Zelator* (London: Century, 1998).
6. Rudolf Steiner, 'The Occult Movement in the Nineteenth Century'—https://wn.rsarchive.org/Lectures/GA254/English/RSP1973/19151018p01.html.
7. Rudolf Steiner, 'The Occult Movement in the Nineteenth Century'—https://wn.rsarchive.org/Lectures/GA254/English/RSP1973/19151018p01.html.
8. Rudolf Steiner, 'The Occult Movement in the Nineteenth Century'—https://wn.rsarchive.org/Lectures/GA254/English/RSP1973/19151018p01.html.
9. Rudolf Steiner, 'The Occult Movement in the Nineteenth Century'—https://wn.rsarchive.org/Lectures/GA254/English/RSP1973/19151018p01.html.

CHAPTER 12

Fusions
(or futures)

Humanity urgently needs to become aware that a spiritual world is working down into every detail of existence in the physical world.

—Rudolf Steiner, *Secret Brotherhoods and the Mystery of the Human Double*

As the last few chapters have attested, there is the growing presence of entropic, or counter-evolutionary, forces within humanity. And these forces have been, and continue to, dominate our reality, which is the nature of the Inversion. It is therefore the responsibility of aware individuals in these times to recognise these forces, attempt to comprehend them, and to transform them into impulses that can work for humankind's evolvement. In this, we need to come to grips with the presence and activity of those aspects deemed as 'evil'. Negative, or entropic, forces are a feature of existence as much as positive, developmental forces. They all act within the playground of attraction, repulsion, and the expression of energy. The Rosicrucians recognised these forces when they referred to the *Deus Inversus*—or the 'Reversed God'. This Reversed God works on humanity through the spheres of evil to counter its development. The Austrian mystic Rudolf Steiner was well aware of the future impact of such forces. He stated that:

> It is essential that the forces which manifest as evil if they appear at the wrong place must be taken in hand ... in such a way that humanity can achieve something with these forces of evil that will be beneficial for the future of the whole of world evolution'.[1]

In this regard, it is important that a person becomes aware of the metaphysical realm that lies beyond the threshold of normal, or everyday consciousness. If we remain unaware of our own forces of spirit-consciousness, then we are more susceptible to the manipulations of such counter-developmental forces. As readers familiar with my previous writings will know, I have attempted to draw attention to certain aspects of our consensus reality in order to gain greater clarity about how we may respond to the situation in a constructive way. I stand by what was written in the Gnostic Gospel of Philip: 'For so long as the root of wickedness is hidden, it is strong. But when it is recognised, it is dissolved. When it is revealed, it perishes'. Recognition, through heightened awareness and perception, brings more choice into play. In the context of the machinic impulse and the intrigues of the Inversion, a person needs to be conscious of certain facts before they can manifest the correct intention and focus of will. What is needed is a culture of revelation—of 'uncovering'—rather than of cover-up.

Conscious life within the Inversion is partly dependent on the fact that the world around us is a delusion. This mode of separation from the Greater Reality has functioned so that the human being can develop their inner world and sense of being—ego consciousness—through free will and action, rather than being a 'plaything of the gods' void of individual vital force or destiny. This phase, it seems, has now served its purpose and it is time to uncover (*reveal*) human spirit-consciousness as a participant in the physical life experience. In order to transform the entropic forces, humanity needs to return to contact with a metaphysical reality. In this respect, the developmental path of humankind has reached a threshold. And to begin crossing that threshold we have to re-experience the world beyond the physical. Humanity needs to be prepared for its next step, which includes the unfolding of new, or hitherto unused, organs of perception. This can only happen if a certain number of individuals can be prepared to initiate this process. New psychic abilities are likely to emerge as a 'thinning of the veils' progresses, the consensus reality increasingly dissolves, and energetic realms begin to cross over. As is already the case now, more and more people are having psychic experiences, such as non-human communications—and this will increase and become more common, unless the entropic forces can drag people further into deepened materialism, which causes amnesia in spirit-consciousness. The important threshold for humanity now is to be receptive to developmental impulses and to consciously open up to a merger, or fusion, with these transcendental forces towards a spiritualised culture.

Referring back to the chapter on Philip K. Dick and his gnostic cosmology (Chapter 3), it was noted how Dick considered that the individual already possessed fragments of the Absolute/Source within them, and that the ultimate goal of a human life was to accomplish this human–Source merger. In Dick's perspective, the Absolute, or Source-of-All (the Urgrund), was all the time penetrating into this false reality construct, and attempting either to trigger/activate people, or waiting for them to arrive at the moment when a merger could be accomplished. If enough people were to assimilate with Source (the merge) then the artificial reality construct (the Inversion) would be annihilated. In its place would be a sentient reality-awareness that is simultaneously all within the Urgrund/Source. Dick also believed that the false god (or 'artefact') is not evil, and neither is the false projected world of the Demiurge (the Inversion). Rather, the Demiurge is deterministic and mechanical and, as such, cannot be appealed to through human values. The Demiurge is itself an artefact that cannot fathom any greater truth beyond itself or purpose for being. Dick's cosmology also recognises the struggle of polarities by saying that the Urgrund/Source, from time to time, gives a revelation to human beings in order to further the positive evolutionary process towards enlightened or perceptual knowing. And to counteract this impulse, the Demiurgic 'false god' entity would induce blindness, forgetfulness, or subterfuge, to further maintain the perceptual darkness. This, argues Dick, is the perpetual struggle that is operative within the lesser reality—what I refer to as the Inversion. In this context, the Source-of-All and humanity is moving toward fusion whereby the artificial construct is moving toward final elimination. It is a feature of Dick's unusual cosmology (which seems a form of neo-gnosticism) that lesser reality is the medium through which the process of the merger between Source and the human being can be actualised.

True Gnostics have felt, in a similar way to Dick, that humanity is 'from elsewhere' and this suggests that we are estranged from our True Reality (the Greater Reality)—on many levels. To assist us in finding 'our way back home' we have the tool of the creative imagination, as well as the mystery wisdom traditions.

The wisdom schools, with their initiates, have also taken on the role of creating conduits for the transmission of real knowledge (i.e. knowledge from outside of the false Inversion construct). Through their work, of which only parts are publicly known, they continue to maintain the lifeline—the umbilical cord—that connects the phenomenal physical world with the realm of Greater Reality. And through this bridge, vital forces can enter this artificial realm and fuse with materiality; that is, to work through physicality. The Initiate Path is a difficult one as the person has to deal with the ego-self in order to prepare the physical body as a vessel for the streaming of transcendental energies. This preparation is sometimes referred to as the 'ego death'—of *dying before you die*—that creates the conduit in allowance for the merger. This is not a channelling but a far more advanced state. The Indian sage Sri Aurobindo put forth a similar notion when he described the supramental consciousness as needing to descend into the physical-material realm through the human being. It is said that the 'Great Work' is to develop individuals to be then sent back out into the society to help facilitate development in their cultural sphere. It is important to produce well-balanced individuals who have developed a degree of immunity against the entropic forces. The more conscious and aware people there are in a community, the less susceptible is that community to external forms of social management and control—i.e. less vulnerable to the Ahrimanic forces of stagnation and decay. The initiate, in this context, is a person who although carries/transmits great power and responsibility, does not wield this power over people in any negative form. This 'Great Work' is ongoing for the contestation between evolvement/de-evolvement is continuous, and this is the situation currently today.

Humankind has moved through various stages necessary for its evolvement; and within this path has been the transition from a condition of spirit-being into earthly, material form. This established a physical separation from spirit-consciousness that activated the human being's growth of ego-self so that it could then return to the state of spirit-being with an individualised awareness. In this, the human being has evolved through the loss of some faculties and the development of others. This has involved a 'descent' from a state of direct consciousness of the metaphysical realms and an ignorance and innocence of the material domain, to a mastery of material forces and a loss of spirit-awareness. The next threshold must involve gaining the correct correspondence and use of material forces alongside a re-spiritualisation of human life within the physical domain. This is the fusion that now stands at humanity's door—and must be taken in hand in an appropriate manner. Otherwise, the momentum of the ascending arc may be missed.

The fusion-merger

We can no longer deny the subverted nature of our reality and the anti-human impulses that are rife in the present earthly life experience. The human being has, on the whole, become far too numbed and desensitised to the atrocities that plague human civilisation. Each day in our news and media channels we hear of terrible human-led crimes, sufferings, and violence; not to mention the absurd behaviour of our political, financial, and corporate systems. So much human activity across the planet would seem like people are asleep within their own nightmares. It is as if human life has slipped within a realm of sub-nature. Humankind is not acting from a correct or balanced place. The madness of the modern world has become normalised as the upside-down Inversion (see Chapter 4). Even in these so-called 'advanced times' our modern societies are predicated upon the energies of sub-nature: oil, gas, coal, etc. The continued proliferation of these denser energies is holding back humanity's development into the sphere of finer forces. As mentioned, even electricity was seen by Steiner as representing sub-natural forces—Ahrimanic forces use the medium of electricity as a vessel. Our electrified world is causing stagnation in the path of humankind's necessary evolution. It is as if the human being is between both worlds—between the suprasensible world (the metaphysical realm) and the sub-sensible world (the denser mechanical realm). In this context, humanity may need to act as a bridge between these polarised forces.

Humanity stands at the threshold between two paths. There is a great risk of falling prey to the mechanical impulse and being incorporated into a dense, technologised world of control, surveillance, and restricted freedoms. This would paradoxically become a sub-natural world of super-technology and 'intelligent' machines. Yet it would be a realm dominated by the Ahrimanic forces that counter the evolutionary impulses within humankind. To work against this, human beings need, as much as possible, to transform the earthly, mechanical impulses into forces for human betterment. And this task requires that the human being attain a level of perception and awareness sufficient to grasp the implications of this situation. In Steiner's words: 'Our age needs knowledge that rises above nature because it must deal inwardly with a dangerous life-content that has sunk below nature'.[2] A period such as we are facing now calls for dedication and commitment; for if not, then the encroaching impulses of apathy, ignorance, and impotence will serve to diminish the human being's receptive capacities. And these receptive capacities are required for the conscious receiving of transcendental impulses—otherwise, they will be turned into mechanical, materialistic efforts. Independent, self-willed perceptive thought (which includes the heart resonance) is necessary for regaining the intuitive insight that once was natural to the human being. Humanity is poised upon this path of potential advancement; only to be hindered by forces that deliberately aim to hold back the species. The choice here is to remain dumbed and numbed—that is, psychologically mummified—by the mainstream mind programming of the dominant consensus reality, or to work quietly and persistently with our personal efforts. Through self-discipline and focused awareness, each person can work to develop their own forms of heightened perception. The decision here is between aligning oneself with those forces that act upon the inner development of the individual and which seek to bring humanity into a merger with Source consciousness; or with the entropic forces that push for selfish, egoistic development. The present work for the human being, I would say, is the acceptance of, and receptivity to, what is called the 'Spirit' (Source consciousness), and to facilitate its emergence through the material realm.

The human being can act as the transformative force in the material world—to be the conductor, as it were, through which higher forces and energies can be transformed down into the physical. We need to resist being overwhelmed by the mechanistic forces of an increasingly technological world. We currently find ourselves enmeshed within an interplay of forces—the controlling forces of sub-nature and the restorative energies of supra-nature (the metaphysical/transcendental). This positioning of the human being between realms has been portrayed also in mythology; the human stands between the realm of the 'gods' and the underworld (the realm of Hades) from where the sub-world dwellers attempt to send out their influences and forces. Humanity has been foretold of its circumstances for many ages, yet the symbolism has been too unclear for many to grasp the significance. The situation now calls for greater awareness and knowledge of these polarised, opposing streams of forces operating within our present reality. And this entails having an understanding of the nature of the Inversion. This has been the reason for the writing of this book. The question is now one of developing the strength of awareness with the receptivity of being open to restorative forces. At the same time, the individual needs to be aware of the nature of negating forces that act upon the world, through societies and cultures, and within people themselves. We cannot transform those forces that we are blind to. And the nature of the Inversion is to perpetuate the sleeping state of blindness. We awaken first with one eye open. As the proverb goes: In the kingdom of the blind, the one-eyed man is king.

It has to be recognised also that the forces of opposition all have a role to serve. It is the friction that creates the potential for movement. Forces that are in opposition may also be serving one another in a way that is not outwardly apparent. Just as a rocket, for example, needs the force of expulsion to propel itself forward (that is, in the opposite direction), so too can the opposing forces work to advance the evolutionary path—*if they are utilised and transformed in the appropriate way*. Here then, the resolution lies in the way of transformation of negating forces. The human being is both *within* the world and *not of* the world. The human being has an origin from beyond the material-physical realms, and yet the consciousness-spirit is taking a sojourn through the human life experience. As such, it has to work with the forces that operate within these spheres of activity. And the activity for the human now is to counteract the entropic forces that are gaining influence through the machinic impulse. In this, a counter impulse must be brought forth through the human being. And what is this counter impulse? Rudolf Steiner already gave the answer to this, which was mentioned in the previous chapter. Steiner stated how the 'Spirits of Form' implanted the principle of *Love* into the of heredity of humankind on Earth. This was a countermeasure against the encroaching forces of mechanism, intellectualism, and the 'head' influences, through which the Ahrimanic forces were largely working. The growth of the Love impulse (not the sentimental version pushed by media representations) must be brought forth through community (fraternity), compassion, empathy, and unselfish goodwill. These values are the foundation that entropic, negating forces cannot penetrate.

The forms and principles through which we live our lives must be attuned to a recognition of spirit-consciousness rather than to be in ignorance of the metaphysical conditions of our life existence. The key feature here is awareness. The entropic, counter-evolutionary forces wish to operate under a veil of unknowing—they do not want that individuals recognise their presence. For this reason, they function through stealth and by proxy. They rarely come out to oppose events directly, for this would shine a light upon their presence. They are shadow beings for they work through the shadows; this includes the dark shadows of our minds, our thoughts (thought-forms), and through our collective shadows. The entropic forces are at home within a rigid, mechanical environment; a world operated by AI, algorithms, data-mining, digital infrastructures, Metaverses, and all forms of computerised realms. These are the artificial realms for us, yet the natural home environment for such anti-human forces. We must be aware of this, and resist falling into their entrapment—of becoming mere pawns or playthings within an electrified prison run by digital-guards, and where the inmates are numbered and catalogued. Those forces that aim to deceive us know full well that if they can get negative emotions to take hold in our hearts, they can block human evolvement. That is why awareness here is so important. Humans are living bodies of transmission; the body is a resonant vessel—a living antenna. If negative emotions, energies, or vibrations take presence within the living body then its capacity to fuse with transcendental impulses is impaired.

The current evolutionary impulse upon this planet is operating through an organic medium. And this includes us. We are carbon-based beings; and yet the carbon-based environment is being turned increasingly hostile against us. Organic food is turning into genetically modified products grown by 'suicide seeds' that unnaturally fail to pass along their heredity. Human reproduction is becoming more and more unnatural as fertility rates plummet across the world. Meat is being grown in labs as livestock is inhumanely treated as lifeless inorganic units. Corporate interests are attempting to persuade people to eat lab-farmed insects. Farms are now mostly factories, and the illness industry is force-fed by corporate Big Pharma. These are blatant signs of the Inversion; so many still remain blind to this, conditioned as they are from birth to accept this normalised madness and delusion. Our perceptions are being hung upside down as we innocently (or ignorantly) prance through life accepting further and further restrictions through techno-cratic, authoritarian control mechanisms. This is not normal, natural, nor organic. This is the path of the machinic impulse, which is the vessel through which the entropic, Ahrimanic forces operate. And it is the same path through which humanity must walk in order to find again its road towards evolvement. The metaphysical presence is within the lesser reality—the Inversion—at all times; yet it has to be acknowledged and recognised in order to be perceived. In this, humanity has to self-awaken its organs of perception. As the wisdom teacher Jalaluddin Rumi stated: 'New organs of perception come into being as a result of necessity. Therefore, O man, increase your necessity, so that you may increase your perception'. The Call has been given on how to proceed within the Inversion.

In his autobiography, Rudolf Steiner wrote: 'The whole world, apart from the human being, is a riddle, the real riddle of existence, and the human being himself is its solution'.[3] This sums up the Inversion entirely—it is a riddle. And the human being must solve the way out of this riddle; the solution resides within. It is as if we are within a dream, and we are being held back from awakening. In the opening prologue of this book, I spoke about the bedtime story we are all told before entering into the sleep of a human life. The dream becomes so captivating and convincing that it causes the dreamer never to awaken. The dreamer continues to dream the dream that they were told before sleeping. We can continue dreaming the wrong dreams; or we can start to dream the right dreams that will lead, eventually, to a morning awakening. Or perhaps this story that I have told within these pages, about the Inversion, has just been another dream to keep you all asleep. Maybe there is no such thing as an Inversion—after all, it sounds a little silly, doesn't it?

And the lullaby comes back to your ears … la la la … sleep a while longer …

Notes

1. Rudolf Steiner, *Secret Brotherhoods and the Mystery of the Human Double*. (Forest Row: Rudolf Steiner Press, 2006), 163.
2. Cited in Sigismund von Gleich, *The Transformation of Evil and the Subterranean Spheres of the Earth*. (Forest Row: Temple Lodge Publishing, 2005), 17.
3. Cited in Sigismund von Gleich, *The Transformation of Evil and the Subterranean Spheres of the Earth*. (Forest Row: Temple Lodge Publishing, 2005), 54.

AFTERWORD

We are now at the point where human culture divides into two streams. Suppose this materialistic way of thinking were to triumph ... the whole of humanity would become mechanized in spirit, vegetative in soul, bestial in body, because the evolution of the Earth leads fatally to that.

—Rudolf Steiner, Stuttgart, 29 June 1919

We need to be awake and discerning. We may have arrived at a point where human culture divides—at least, cognitively speaking. A great deceit is being played out within our current consensus reality. The great deceit that is coming upon us is the unveiling of a so-called 'utopia' based upon the isolation of the human spirit-consciousness. This fake promise is wrapped up in tech-salvationist terms, heralding a false ideal future. The real dis-ease of the human condition is to be in a state of estrangement. That is, estranged and alienated from any metaphysical influence or nourishment. It is not that the metaphysical background to life must necessarily be obvious to us, or tangible in our daily lives—only that we are cognisant of its existence and continual influence. Yet once this sense of recognition (the act of aware cognition) is dissolved, a barren soulless life is the result. And yet, in most circumstances, people will not be cognisant of this loss—this lack of the transcendental impulse in their lives—for they will be entrained into a reality consisting of a physical-digital mesh that keeps them attached to their lower nature and desires. This deceit consists of a most heinous form of enslavement, for it shall both be a willing one as well as an ignorant one. The splintering of the human being from its metaphysical connection shall go almost unnoticed, and the transfer into a reality of limited consciousness will have been enacted quite skilfully. This sly route to a human condition of alienation, procured through the guise of technological advancement and progress, will be a coup against the creative spirit. And this shall be the *reversal* of the human reality.

The almost imperceptible dangers are that we have been slipping into a *reversed reality* (the Inversion), constructed through a realm of fantasy and make-believe, which now fuels the crass and superficial culture industries that dominate modern life. Any notion of Higher Reality has been twisted into an artificial lesser reality, dissociating humankind not only from its natural, organic, carbon-based environment, but also from an inherent contact with its origin—Source consciousness. If anyone wishes to see how 'signals' can operate within the Inversion, then watch all the episodes in the recent *Westworld* TV series (2016–2022). In Season Four, the machinic android 'hosts' have taken control of the world using a bioengineered virus that infects humans over the course of a generation, turning them docile and susceptible to AI and 'host' control. Storylines and narratives are created in order to give people their roles and characters in life, which they passively follow believing them to be their own life stories. Humankind is managed through these manufactured 'storylines' (aka socio-cultural narratives) that are transmitted directly to the minds and lives of humans through a series of radio-sonic transmission signals via the global technological infrastructure.

Of course, this is just a story after all, isn't it? It is just fantasy and make-believe. The world is not really like that—not at all. Luckily, once the television fantasy is finished and the device is put on standby mode, we can return to our 'normal' lives. Long ago we were told that parts of humanity are living in a 'rebellious house' with eyes that do not see and ears that do not hear (Ezekiel 12:2). This ignorance was the consequence of living within such a 'rebellious house' (aka the Inversion). We now have the partial awareness to make the necessary choices. We can alter our perception of this reversed reality by choosing to seek to expand our own state of cognition. In doing so, our perceptions change and that allows us to change. We can intentionally improve our perceptual abilities. We can choose to exercise our discernment. We can either take a step forward or remain where we are. As always, the choice remains with us.

The story of the dreaming continues ... will you open your eyes?

Yes, the world is an illusion. But Truth is always being shown there.
—Idries Shah, *The Dermis Probe*.

REFERENCES

Berardi, F. (2021). *The Third Unconscious*. London: Verso.

Berman, M. (1990). *Coming to Our Senses: Body and Spirit in the Hidden History of the West*. New York: HarperCollins.

Dennis, K. (2019). *Healing the Wounded Mind: The Psychosis of the Modern World and the Search for the Self*. Forest Row: Clairview Books.

Dennis, K. (2021). *Hijacking Reality: The Reprogramming & Reorganization of Human Life*. Leicester: Beautiful Traitor Books.

Dick, P. K. (1995). *The Shifting Realities of Philip K. Dick: Selected Literary and Philosophical Writings* (ed. Lawrence Sutin). New York: Vintage Books.

Emberson, P. (2013). *Machines and the Human Spirit*. Scotland: The DewCross Centre for Moral Technology.

Grosse, E. J. (2021). *Are There People Without A Self?* Forest Row: Temple Lodge.

Harrison, C. G. (2021). *The Transcendental Universe*. London: Azafran Books.

Hedsel, M. (1998). *The Zelator*. London: Century.

Hoeller, S. A. (2014). *The Gnostic Jung and the Seven Sermons to the Dead*. Wheaton: Quest Books.

Horsley, J. (2004). *The Lucid View: Investigations into Occultism, Ufology, and Paranoid Awareness*. Illinois: Adventures Unlimited.

Horsley, J. (2018). *Prisoner of Infinity: UFOs, Social Engineering, and the Psychology of Fragmentation*. London: Aeon Books.

Huxley, A. (1959). *Brave New World Revisited*. London: Chatto & Windus.

Jung, C. G. (2010). *The Undiscovered Self (with Symbols and The Interpretation of Dreams)*. Princeton: Princeton University Press.

Kalsched, D. (1996). *The Inner World of Trauma: Archetypal Defences of the Personal Spirit*. London: Routledge.

Laing, R. D. (1990). *The Politics of Experience & The Bird of Paradise*. London: Penguin Books.

Lash, J. L. (2006). *Not In His Image: Gnostic Vision, Sacred Ecology, and the Future of Belief*. Vermont: Chelsea Green Publishing.

Leary, T. (1988). *Info-Psychology*. New Mexico: New Falcon Publications.

Lilly, J. C. (1972). *Programming and Metaprogramming in THE HUMAN BIOCOMPUTER*. New York: The Julien Press.

Lilly, J. C. (1988). *The Scientist: A Metaphysical Autobiography*. Berkeley: Ronin Publishing.

Noble, D. F. (1999). *The Religion of Technology: The Divinity of Man and the Spirit of Invention*. London: Penguin.

Ouspensky, P. D. (1950). *In Search of the Miraculous: Fragments of an Unknown Teaching*. London: Routledge & Kegan Paul.

Perlas, N. (2018). *Humanity's Last Stand: The Challenge of Artificial Intelligence—A Spiritual-Scientific Response*. Forest Row: Temple Lodge.

Steiner, R. (1973). *Anthroposophical Leading Thoughts* (trans. George and Mary Adams). London: Rudolf Steiner Press.

Steiner, R. (2006). *Secret Brotherhoods and the Mystery of the Human Double*. Forest Row: Rudolf Steiner Press.

Steiner, R. (2008). *The Fall of the Spirits of Darkness*. Forest Row: Rudolf Steiner Press.

Steiner, R. (2009). *The Incarnation of Ahriman: The Embodiment of Evil on Earth*. Forest Row: Rudolf Steiner Press.

Steiner, R. (2011). *Knowledge of the Higher Worlds*. Forest Row: Rudolf Steiner Press.

Upton, C. (2021). *The Alien Disclosure Deception: The Metaphysics of Social Engineering*. Sophia Perennis.

Vallee, J. (2015). *The Invisible College: What a Group of Scientists Has Discovered About UFO Influences on the Human Race*. Charlottesville: Anomalist Books.

von Gleich, S. (2005). *The Transformation of Evil and the Subterranean Spheres of the Earth*. Forest Row: Temple Lodge Publishing.

Zuboff, S. (2019). *The Age of Surveillance Capitalism: The Fight for a Human Future at the New Frontier of Power*. London: Profile Books.

ABOUT THE AUTHOR

KINGSLEY L. DENNIS, PhD, is a full-time writer and researcher. He previously worked in the Sociology Department at Lancaster University, UK. Kingsley is the author of numerous articles on social futures; technology and new media communications; global affairs; and conscious evolution. He is the author of over 20 books including *Life in the Continuum*; *UNIFIED: Cosmos, Life, Purpose*; *Hijacking Reality*; *Healing the Wounded Mind*; *The Modern Seeker*; *Bardo Times*; *Breaking the Spell*; *New Consciousness for a New World*, and *Dawn of the Akashic Age* (with Ervin Laszlo). Kingsley also runs his own publishing imprint, Beautiful Traitor Books (www.beautifultraitorbooks.com). For more information, visit his website: www.kingsleydennis.com.

INDEX

Printed in the USA
CPSIA information can be obtained
at www.ICGtesting.com
JSHW010934241123
52664JS00014B/120